AF490427

WHAT DO ANIMALS TALK ABOUT?

STORIES, ESSAYS AND PLAYS

TENZING RAPGYAL

Copyright © Tenzing Rapgyal
All Rights Reserved.

This book has been self-published with all reasonable efforts taken to make the material error-free by the author. No part of this book shall be used, reproduced in any manner whatsoever without written permission from the author, except in the case of brief quotations embodied in critical articles and reviews.

The Author of this book is solely responsible and liable for its content including but not limited to the views, representations, descriptions, statements, information, opinions and references ["Content"]. The Content of this book shall not constitute or be construed or deemed to reflect the opinion or expression of the Publisher or Editor. Neither the Publisher nor Editor endorse or approve the Content of this book or guarantee the reliability, accuracy or completeness of the Content published herein and do not make any representations or warranties of any kind, express or implied, including but not limited to the implied warranties of merchantability, fitness for a particular purpose. The Publisher and Editor shall not be liable whatsoever for any errors, omissions, whether such errors or omissions result from negligence, accident, or any other cause or claims for loss or damages of any kind, including without limitation, indirect or consequential loss or damage arising out of use, inability to use, or about the reliability, accuracy or sufficiency of the information contained in this book.

Made with ♥ on the Notion Press Platform
www.notionpress.com

To my beautiful family: Lobsang Dolma, my wife; Kunga Tashi Basil and Kunga Tsehla Basil, my children for making me a complete man.

To my late genuine popo who I extorted money from when I was in school and college, but I could not repay him with true interest.

To my pala, who till we were secure in our professional life, worked tirelessly till he went to bed like a dead log on the road side near a dumping area.

To my brother for the musical environment which motivated me to pick up drumsticks.

To my friend, Ngawang Palden, for his friendship when I was an alien in Chandigarh for education and later when I was a stranger in Dharmashala for job.

And lastly, my ama for her sacrifice.

Contents

Contents

Preface

Writing for me has been an outlet to express my self. I have compiled my thoughts, emotions, imaginations and visions captured in words in different forms to share with my you.

Some of the pieces are spontaneous. Some are exerted. Some are cathartic. Some are philosophical. Some are mundane. Some are political. Some are personal. Some are argumentative. Some are trite.

The 'I' in this book is not completely me.

Prologue

" To me, the true artist is one who lives completely, harmoniously, who does not divide his art from living, whose very life is that expression, whether it be a picture, music, or his behavior; who has his expression on a canvas or in music or in stone from his daily conduct, daily living. That demands the highest intlligence, highest harmony. To me the true artist is the man who has that harmony. He may express it on canvas, or he many talk, or he may paint; or he may not exprss it at all, he may feel it. But this demands that exquisite pose, that intensity of awareness and, therefore, his expression is not divorced from the daily continuty of living."

J.Krishnamurti, Total Freedom: The Essential Krishnamurti

Acknowledgements

I am grateful to my wife for letting me have a sound sleep at nights even when our children in infancy and even now wake up due to fever, cold, diarrhea, thunder, lighntening and so on so that I can go to bed late to mull, muse and muster to write and read and to wake up fresh in the morning to go to work to play the roles of an educator, a police, a counsellor, an advisor, a stand up comedian, a singer, a pubic speaking coach, a script writer, a director, a life coach, a father, a brother, a friend, a puncing bag and many more to my lovely students and to enact the same roles to my children after work with my wife, who have similar roles being in the same profession.

I could not have been a writer without her publicly and personally unappreciated support.

I am thankful to have two beautiful children who convince me everday that life is a miracle when I see them transforming from this puking pumpkin to piping hot headed cacophonous cute cunning monsters.

CHAPTER ONE

The Lost Poem

I miss the lost poem which I wrote on a wrinkled a piece of paper when I saw gnarling rotting roots of a tree exposed from the side of an eroded mound at a pilgrimage site in Nepal. I had saved the paper in a book I was reading. But I don't remember what book it was. I am not sure if the book is in my collection on the shelf.

I said to my mom, " *Pala* is concerned about you."

"Really, did he talk to you about me?"

"Yes, he did."

"When he is here he does not speak. He reads the scripture and counts the rosary.

"But he is concerned about you. He told me on our way back home."

There was silence between us.

I visited her every day. I would sit near her at her feet talking to her or reading something. Leaving her by herself at night was difficult for me. But we did not have any choice.

When I get close to her to hug, she would move back and say, "Don't come near me. I smell." Yes she did. Yet I would tell her that she did not.

She would constipate and would ask me to insert a laxative in her rectum. It did not disgust me but saddened me.

Even though the pain was unbearable, she never complained to me. She never cried in my presence. She would wince with pain though.

On our way back home one evening, I asked my pala why it was not diagnosed earlier. He said they did but my mom did not take it seriously.

I asked my mother the same question. She said, "What is the point of it? How could we afford the treatment? How could *pala* manage it? I asked her, "Why did not you tell me when I came home on holiday?" Her answer was that she did not want to disrupt my studies.

So, I had no idea about her condition until the last stage.

After one week, I had to go back to work in Dharamsala. He told me how once in our maternal uncle's presence our mother bled from her breast and he did nothing but shied away from the spot.

After a month or so, on an evening while I was taking round of the classes during students' self-study hour, I got a call from my father who said in a matter of fact tone, " Your mother died in my presence today. I poured the holy water in her mouth in her last breath. He assured me, " Don't worry. I will not bring any step mother." I felt a lump in my throat and a relief for her. I walked up and around the school building to monitor the students' self-study of 60 minutes as if nothing has happened to me.

She was free from the pain.

I remember lying to her that she would be cured.

I remember the sense of helplessness of leaving her alone at night in the corridor of the government hospital as no male attendants were allowed and our female relatives only gave a cursory visit a couple of times during the day time. The doctors had advised pala not to waste money on her treatment. So, she was left in the corridor not on the bed in a ward in the hospital to die.

I remember her bald head, sunken eyes, hollow cheeks, bony hands, shrunken legs and her faint smile on the parched lips.

I remember feeling the ridges of her spinal cord when I hugged and caressed her back.

I remember every time I left her after the visiting hours, my heart broke and eyes tore. Once I ran into a female relative at the entrance of the hospital. When she saw my red eyes, I ran away from her with a suffocating lump in my throat.

I don't remember the poem clearly.

I worry about my daughter even though she is just 5 years old.

CHAPTER TWO

Doon Valley To Delhi Belly

The sky was overmasted. I grumbled her, "Why is it that it rains whenever we leave for Delhi? Last time too we had a rainy farewell.

It started to pour down. So, we couldn't wait for the bus on the highway to ISBT. I called up one of the taxi drivers. We didn't get any taxi service because of Indra Dev's interruption.

So, we waited in silence in the chatter of the rain.

Thankfully, the god pressed the pause button. We walked up the narrow street to the highway and waited for the public transport with luggage slung across my shoulder. My t-shirt was drenched in sweat.

Finally.......the bus arrived after waiting with impatience and irritation for half an hour. When the bus moved, the cool breeze through the rickety windows was refreshing and soothing. I thanked Vayu Dev!

We boarded Volvo around 2:30 in the afternoon. Since, the ticket would be reimbursed; we opted for the deluxe service. Otherwise, I would have preferred the ordinary bus service as it was not so hot due to the rain. Ordinary buses are well ventilated whereas Volvos are suffocating, for the air is conditioned.

The smell of the bus was inducing nausea in my wife's throat. She demanded Kurkure with bitterness written all over her face. I meekly and lovingly fetched a packet in hurry. After some time, we were jolted out of our sleep; we had travelled for two hours. We were hungry. We unpacked our lunch made from the leftovers in the fridge. Usually, I don't like home made food eating out. I like eating out when I am out.

The bus at last took a halt at Haldiram's and McDonald's. There was the temptation to bite into chicken burger. However, we were full. My wife wanted to have tea because it was the tea time at home. I looked around, but there was none. Not a single road side tea stall. How can they compete with the giants who have conquered the westernized taste buds? With frustration, she begged, "Can't we have tea at Haldiram's? I curtly remarked, "No, it is very expensive. They fleece 25 Rupees more for the same cup of road side well brewed tea." She was not convinced by my pseudo-leftist argument. I suggested cold lemon tea, cold bottled milk, ice cream...... She wanted a hot cup of sweet tea. We went to the recess room in cold war. In the end, I give in and asked her if I should get a cup of Haldiram tea for her. She just nodded in rejection. And the bus honked its horn.

When I looked out of the window, many stretch of fields with lush crops passed by without any interruption. I thought to myself, "Where do these crops go? How come there is shortage of food in India?" It was just a rhetorical question. I knew the answer.

The trees were fresh and green.

As we neared Delhi, the tsunami of humanity was drawing in. Being in hills most of my life congested Delhi knocks me down with its cold, heat, humidity and humanity.

We got down at Vaishali as we were heading towards Lobsang's sister's place. My sister-in-law lives in Laxmi Nagar. It 9:00 in the evening. It was Monday. Next day, I went to Lajpat Nagar at the Bureau of H.H.The Dalai Lama to renew my IC (Identity Certificate provided by the Indian Government to Tibetan Refugees). When I got there it was quarter to 2. The gatekeeper did not allow me to get in pointing his long index finger at the notice which said that they don't deal with public after 1:30. I pleaded him to let me in. He said he couldn't, it was his duty. He suggested me to come back after 2:30 when some staff from the IC section go to the passport office so that I could request them to consider my request.

I had paronthas with chole at a road side food stall. The bread was not moist. How can they be in such a heat? They can't sweat like us.

I went back to him. With my stomach full with the food and acidity, I once again urged him to allow me in. I tried to convince him that I had to just drop in my application forms. That's all. He did not give in and commented, "It is bureaucracy, my friend. You will find this hurdle in Indian as well as Tibetan offices." He was right. He was doing his job. I liked him.

I patiently waited at the gate. A woman in late 30s appeared, the gate keeper indicated me. I approached her to put my request forward to her. In a patronizing tone, she said, "Why don't you respect the rules of this office? The Bureau is like an embassy. Would you do the same thing in other embassies? Will they listen to you?" I thought she made a lot of sense, but what about my problem: why can't I just drop in and hand in my application. The kind gate keeper advised me to hang on. Another official came out, I hesitatingly closed in to her and told her, "Madam, I have to submit my application. I did not know the rule. It has been two years since I last visited here. I can't come tomorrow because we have to attend workshop." She listening patiently to me said, "Oh, you are going to attend the workshop organized by NCERT. Since you are a government employee, I will let you in but we should respect our rules, you know." I thanked her profusely for abetting in braking the rule.

When the work was done, I was in time for the reporting at NCERT guest house. As usual the metro was overcrowded. I get intimidated to get down at Rajiv Chowk. I usually get crushed in the clash of human tide. When I am sandwiched between the squeezing in and out, my main concern is to feel my pockets for my mobile phone and the purse.

CHAPTER THREE

I Am An Owl

I go for evening walk after dinner for digestion to the market nearby. The sidewalk has become a parking lot. So, getting to the market gives you some mental exercise for alertness. On the roadside there is a juice shop: under the bright bulb and a small busy fan, the sweating man is surrounded by the colorful fruits. We routinely have a glass of shake with a scoop of ice cream topped with some dry fruits. In Dehradun, we don't get the quantity and the quality at the price he charges.

As we enter the market, our attention is drawn to the shop which sells branded clothes. Their bait is the discounts. As a language teacher, what is interesting is the usage of preposition-'up to'. Even though we know what they are up to, we fall into it.

The other day, Dorjee, my roommate from Spiti, had a haircut in the market. I hung around the maze of shops, bought a trunk, as I forget to pack another for change and hand some boiled eggs, as I am addicted to having it at breakfast every day; but, at the guest house, we get it occasionally. However, I don't have any complain about it. My stay here has been intellectually stimulating and gastronomically satisfying.

While coming back, he told me that the barber asked him what my religion is. It rang the bell in my mind. I knew why he asked him that question. He told me what he replied to him. I asked him what his name was. He was a mussalman, who might have thought that we were brothers of the same faith because of my goatee. I have noticed the inquiring eyes of men wearing the skull cap and the beard and women in burka on bus, in biryani shops, in places near mosques...In my hometown, Darjeeling; I am often mistaken for a nepali due to my high bridged nose. And the most amusing mistaken identity was a helper in NCERT asking me if I was a Jat from Haryana, as there is Kuljeet Singh from Spiti on the list of the participants at the workshop. When I am in an expensive restaurant, the waiter believes that I am from South-east Asia. Sometimes, my origin is Manipur in the northeast of India. I used to get annoyed at the fact that people don't know that there are Tibetans in Asia who also have squinted eyes. But, I have learned to be amused by it. Do I have any other choice? Last Saturday, in a restaurant, while ordering kofta, I overheard someone sitting next to us remarking to the other in low voice, "Yehlog kuchbhi katey hai." The statement implies snakes, cockroaches, worms, frogs, dogs, monkeys...COWS. With a restrained anger, I tried to educate him, "All the people with mongoloid features are not only from Manipur. You need to get out of Dehli. Explore the world my friends." Later I thought he might not have known what being racist meant. We just became an interesting topic for them to pass their time while waiting for their order.

Day before yesterday, on our way back to the campus from the market, a man was staggering in front of us on the busy highway. I wonder if he reached home safely. There was a police van on the road side. I thought they would do something about it, but they seemed to enjoy his wobbly gait. I kept looking back at him till he faded in the rush on the road. Did he end up in hospital or home? I hope for the latter.

Above the intertwined swans of NCERT, the pithy philosophy reads Knowledge till Death. I hope I have not lost anything in translation as my friend has not studied Sanskrit. Similarly but with a vast difference in implication, a Tibetan master once said, "We should acquire knowledge even if we are dying tomorrow. Even if you don't become a scholar this life, like in a bank, you have deposited your wealth of knowledge for your next life."

I asked myself which one is better. In essence both convey the same message. But I prefer the former, even though I am a proud Buddhist, for its secular context. This is the delicate thread which holds this amazing country full of contradictions. Gandhi wove this thread in his charkha.

Whenever, I pass by the logo, I try to utter those words fluently. I still falter at the last word. It is quiet complicated.

CHAPTER FOUR

At 5

A friend of mine said, “My eyes get sleepy when they see the first rays of sunlight in the horizon.” Every one of us laughed. We knew he spent his sleepless nights roaming well planned paths of Chandigarh hunting hot parantha vendors and sweet tea and wandering in the maze of newspapers which we would find sprawling in his room. He would sleep when the sun rose. He was an extremist in that sense.

We ordinary mortals went to bed around 2:00 a.m and woke up around 10:a.m. ‘Around’ not ‘At’ because we followed our peripatetic hearts not the precision of time. Around 10, when the door was slapped, I would wake up to unlatch and turn back to the bed with blurry eyes smelling hot paronthas with melting butter and scrambled eggs. When the room was filled with the flavor and the long fast needed to be broken, the right hand would stretch out to fetch the breakfast on the messy coffee table and then the body would erect itself; eyes still half asleep and the mouth and the nose would be busy relishing the morning Punjabi nourishment.

After taking a quick shower, I would head to the college. The class would start at 11.Back from the college around 2 in the afternoon; it is lunch time in the hostel mess. With a heavy meal, a long siesta would ensue. Tea and snacks around 5. And then hanging out with friends in the Sector 17 market is a tribal ritual. Seldom would we have lunch at the mess. Eating out is an essential part of hanging out. Else, what else would we do? Back to the room around 10 would lead us to meditate through the day's newspaper. The most important section of the news paper was the entertainment page to check what is on in cinema halls. We would keenly wait for first day first show on Friday. When the contemplation on corruption and violence in the world is over, some would just laze around looking up and around and into one another until they dozed into sleep; I would read some books till 1 to 1:30 and next morning I would find my book in my bed when the waft of hot breakfast would knock on my door. Sometimes, we would be awakened in the middle of the night by the bearded tall lanky gun trotting police. We would just look at you and around you and leave with an air of authority and power.

I continued to be an owl later in my professional life too.

In the school where I started my teaching career, the class commenced late and ended early. Afternoon was for swimming in the river and taking a long nap. There was a lot of time to read a lot. Apart from wasting time, I learned Tibetan language, history and culture, religion, and current affairs for Fulbright scholarship. In addition, I did for M.A in Economics. I was into music too when my younger brother was sent to Dharamsala from Darjeeling to be connected to and surrounded with authentic Tibetan people and culture. After dinner, having kept abreast of the news and views and been entertained with cheap comedies, reading routine precedes before going to sleep around 1:00 to wake up at 7:30 sparing enough time to be at work at 9:00.

The routine resumed in my previous school after I jumped off the launching pad except that the afternoon was occupied till 4:00; sometimes it would extend to 6-7 when I was elected with co-curricular responsibilities. During one month summer time table when the class starts at 7:30, the owl would have a day mare. However, a short nap after class at 4 was never missed or disturbed in the lonely building surrounded by silent trees away from the noisy playground. The night would start at 10:00 when the drums had been beaten in the R-59 band; the dinner had been cooked in the kitchen and consumed in front of T.V. One hour would be devoted to cacophonous T.V discussion and two hours before hitting the bed would be spent on reading, and waking up at 7:30 to continue the morning ritual with enough time to be at the assembly on time. The routine went on for 4 years until our son schemed to bring us together to be born after 5 years. My late to rise period was over but early to bed was still in a distant future. But the much desired happy nappy wasn't gone.

In the middle of 2011, I landed up in the land of dust in Doon valley. It is very hot and humid here in Spring and Summer. To avoid the afternoon heat, the class ends at 1:30 which means the school starts early at 7:15, which means waking up latest by 6. In the beginning, afternoon nap around 4 for 30 to 60 minutes followed by tea and snacks, succeeded by playing the guitar for an hour and the drum for an hour, going for a stroll, having dinner around 8, watching T.V, reading and being alone with a book before the eyes drop around 1:00 went smoothly until our life revolved around our sun.

When he comes back from the crèche our room rumbles. Trying to nap is a concentrated effort to shut one's ears away from his shouts. Going to bed early turned out to be many failed experiments as forcing my eyes to drop would drag the sleepless state till the accustomed time to sleep. Going to bed early seemed like giving away my freedom to indulge in reading, pondering and enjoying my own company for two to three hours. It had been a struggle until I saw a TED talk by a young entrepreneur who shared the advantages of waking up at 4. Now days, I reluctantly wake up at 5, write for half an hour, prepare breakfast, have tea, pack my tiffin, freshen up and go to work around 7. At night, the room calms around 9 when our son settles down to sleep. I read till 10. Sometimes it stretches to 10:30 with the nagging thoughts in the back of mind reminding me the importance of sleeping for at least 7 hours.

I have given up daily doses of T.V discussions, Rig's Restoration, Count Custom and Pawn Shop. I hardly practice the drums and the guitar. I have stopped working in the afternoon to clean our room before Kunga returns from the crèche. When he is around, there is chaos. The best thing is I get half an hour to write 150 to 200 words in the morning every day. Like reading, writing has become a part of my habit.

I set the alarm at 5, but have not been alarmed out of bed till 5:30 or 6:00 with a heavy head. I am going to bed 2 hours earlier and waking up 1 hour earlier, which means I have added one more hour to my sleep. I sleep for 6 to 7 hours compared to 5 to 6 hours earlier. I get time to shower before going to work. I get time to drink tea with leisure not while preparing breakfast.

I will wake up at 5. It is a gradual process. No alarming rate. No magical transformation. Evolution takes time.

Today is 26th of July, 2016 and the word count is 191 in 30 minutes.

CHAPTER FIVE

Po Po

"Tenzin....Tenzin, aren't you coming for lunch!!", screamed my popo through the barred window at a distance while I was playing with my friends in the dumping area behind the street where my parents sold clothes for living. Irritated by the persistent call in Kham accent, I told my Nepali friends, " Look my fake grand pa is calling me."

I still carry the image of walking with him holding his big rough hand looking up to his tall frame talking to him.

I still feel the guilt of taking money from him while I was in school and college because he was an aging bachelor with no blood relatives in India, earned his livelihood at a meager salary working in Economic Hardware Store.

I still remember the old tin trunk he would drag from under the messy bed where I spent a lot of lonely time suffused with the air of incense coming from the bright alter lined with the bowls of water offered to Buddha and other gods.

I still remember jesting about his looking like the inimitable Bollywood Don, Mucambo: broad cheekbone, long face with big ridge and large lips.

He was very short tempered. Once my mother had an argument with him over something and I remember urging her to stop. Later she often teased me for siding with him rather than her!

When my younger brother got job, we decided to send him money every month, but he refused. Even though I feel indebted to him, I have not been sincere enough to repay his kindness. We were hardly in touch with one another. After our father came to Dharamsala to live with us, he was left alone at the old age home in Darjeeling.

In Nepal in 2005, we were on pilgrimage. I remember him boasting of his robust health to a fellow pilgrim. I heard him saying, “I’m 80 years old.” We were climbing down a steep hill where it is believed that one of the incarnations of Buddha sacrificed his body to a hungry tigress.

And in 2011, after a gap of six years, my father and younger brother went to Darjeeling to take him to Bodhgaya on another pilgrimage. But, he was bed ridden. He couldn’t move as he confined himself in his room immersed in reading holy texts. He was brought to Dharamsala and looked after in my brother’s tiny house where his wife, 2 years old son and pala live. Since he was a self respecting person, he felt uncomfortable being a burden to them. So, with great difficulty running from pillars to posts, in the end, pa la got him admission in the old age home in Dharamsala

Later that year, during Winter holiday, as Pala was going to Bodhgaya, I brought him to my place in Dehradun to look after him for a month. I feel fortunate to get that opportunity. However, I realized the cruelty of senility. The significance of the last line of Shakespeare’s Stages of Life struck me during that time. Remorse gnaws me as I was cruel to him because I was so frustrated to see him helpless like an infant.

Now, he is released from his shrinking cage.

Astrological consultations assured us that he will be reborn as a human if the necessary pujas are performed for the departed soul. I prefer to believe that even though I am skeptical.

CHAPTER SIX

I Was Not Like This Before

I stretched my hands to hug him. Smiling at him I put myself between his extended arms. I held him tight but he did not. I think he did not intend to hug me. He was in the veranda stretching his arms and legs with his back leaned against the wash basin.

It was winter. I was in Dharamsala at my brother's place.

Pala was going to Bodhgaya on pilgrimage with his friend, who is older than him and goes there every year. His children are abroad. He lives in a tiny room alone in Dharamsala. Pala had called me to look after PoPo at my place for a month during my winter vacation in Dehradun, as Pala took care of him. My younger brother couldn't as he and his wife had to go to work and they had Dhondhen, their son, to take care of. Dhonden was a delight to be with: the power house of innocent energy. He is the first member of the second generation of our family in exile. The second is coming at the end of this year or the beginning of the next year.

We saw Pala off with his friend in McLeod Ganj. The following night around eight Popo and I left for Dheradun. It was very cold. On the way Popo wanted to pee. I told him to pee in the diaper he was wearing. After some time he said, "Tenzin, I want to pee." I snapped at him, " Pee in the diaper or hold till the bus stops for break." After a few moments, he said, "Tenzin, I want to pee." I just kept quiet swooning with irritation. At last the bus halted for tea. He climbed down the bus with great difficulty. There was no toilet around. So, I took him at a corner in dark, unbelted his pants and unstrapped his diaper. He peed between his thin shivering legs. I felt a sudden gust of sadness for him. I was in hurry to strap him up, but I did not know how to fix the diaper. I was a struggle for both him and me fighting off the biting wind.

Finally we reached Dehradun. It was wee hours. There were no souls except that of rickshaw wallas hunting for the travelling souls to get them to their destinations. There was no place to sit on. PoPo was staggering. I took him to the narrow lane lined with shuttered shops. I asked him to lean against one of the closed shops while I went to get our luggage from the dickey in irritation as the conductor was shouting at me to hurry up. There were three bags which I hung around by body and ran towards PoPo, who seemed to be losing his balance.

We hired an auto rickshaw after much ritualistic haggling. Wind rushed through the openings of the vehicle on all sides. PoPo seemed to feel cold. I asked him. He just nodded in negative. I held his sinewy hands. They were cold. It wished the distance to my place had shortened. When we entered my place after 50 minutes' noisy engine enabled journey from the bus station, PoPo's face lightened up in the warmth of the room. He sat on the bed while I made broth of barley flour. He savored the steam stew. He wanted to pee. I took him to the toilet. He smiled and said that I had an attached toilet, which is very convenient. He said at my brother's place, the toilet is at a distance. So, Pala attends him at home.

The following month passed waking up every morning with headaches, as PoPo moves a lot while asleep which leaves him uncovered with the quilt, so he has to pee after an hour or two because of cold and his bladder to too old to hold pee. In the beginning, he called me when had to pee, but later he did not, for he sensed my irritation. So, he would struggle to get out of the bed. Since I slept on the floor beside his bed, he would step on me and I would wake up to fetch the container and hold it for him to pee. Many a times, there is no pee even though he felt the sensation. So, he grunts to force the pee out, but he would get tired. He would get irritated. He would say, "I was not like this before." Many a times, pee gets out of the way into his pants as a result of miss fitting the container to the source.

He had to be looked after like an infant day and night. It was a matter of concern for me to go out for shopping for long. Usually I shopped at Dhoolkot village, but once I went to the main market and when I came back after an hour or two, the room was stinking. I smelled around, looked at him with a sniffing face. He was as usual in his sedative mode. I asked him if he shitted in his pants. He said that he went to the toilet. I switched on the light and saw the trail of yellowish clawed stains on the floor and the wall which opens to the kitchen. I followed the mark to the toilet where the tiles were smeared in the same style. In irritation, I stormed back to popo's bed and removed his blanket to look for the evidence. There it was: his socks were hidden under the bed and underpants along the corner of the bed against the wall. Both of them were wet and smelly. In fury, I pulled him out of the bed and dragged him to the toilet naked and splashed many jugs of water against his buttock and groin. His legs shivered. He protested my ablution attack resulting in my giving him some smarting spanking on his sagging behind. When cleaning abuse was done, as I was putting some clothes on him, he pointed at the wet underpants, which he had tried to clean in water in the toilet. I told him it was dirty, but he said it was washed clean. Later that night I felt very guilty.

After a week, we got used to one another. We understood one another. I got used to the routine: waking up late, getting him to brush his teeth and wash his face in basin in his bed with a plastic sheet spread on his lap, waiting for him to pee, preparing breakfast, feeding him, taking him out for walk, coming back to room, taking some rest, cleaning the room, watching T.V, cooking lunch, feeding him, taking a nap, waking up, brewing tea, watching T.V, preparing dinner, eating, watching T.V, talking with him, going to bed, waiting for him pee 5 or 6 times a night, waking up late............

But once, at night, he woke me up to remove his blanket. It was very cold, so I had covered him with extra blanket. I got so angry that I removed the entire blanket and the quilt leaving him to fend himself against the cold. There was stillness of silence in the room. After sometime, popo said, "Tenzin, don't do this. I am felling cold." I said, "It is better this way. You don't listen to me. You need to keep yourself warm and you want the blanket to be removed. How many times have you shitted in your pants? Your stomach is running." "Tenzin, don't do this."

When I see a trotting baby, it reminds me of him-his staggering walk around the school football ground holding my hand. Popo, you still live in my memory.

CHAPTER SEVEN

I Waited For Fifeteen Years

It was getting dark and birds were tweeting in the nests and insects were chatting in the holes. We were at the Spring Water. The scarcity of water in Darjeeling had driven us closer to nature. Jerkins were waiting quietly with their mouth open beneath the busy gush of spring through a rusted pipe.

I was hesitant to express my dream to my father. I was home with B.A. I had planned to pursue M.A and PhD. But I knew the reality of our financial situation. Moreover, my younger brother was going to college as he had passed senior secondary school exam. He too needed financial support.

However, I said to him, " Pala,..... I .....want to continue my ....further studies." There was a silence filled with chirping and cricketing and gushing.

"How long?

"Atleast two years. But more for further education."

" I can't support you for two years."

" How about one year professional course? It is a must these days to get a job."

"How long is Teacher Training?

"One year"

"Do teacher training. It is a noble profession. People respect them and they get paid well. If you are willing, I will try."

I never thought of being a teacher. I did not want to be a teacher though I had a knack for teaching as I used to teach my friends in hostel who needed help. I was thinking of rather doing a diploma in computer application, but I did not tell him.

"O.K"

I was with my friend back in Chandigarh for post graduation. My strategy was to fail in the entrance exam so that I could be at the lower rung of the IT world in future. So, I sat for the exam without any preparation. When the result came out, to my surprising dismay, I passed the test and was eligible for admission to be trained as a teacher. Was it predestined, a fate or by chance? Or was it a cosmic joke?

After a rigorous training of one year with, of course, no less amount of self-indulgence, I became a qualified teacher and applied for jobs at various institutions like T.C.V, Sambhota School and Transit School. I got accepted to teach in the capacity of a PRT at Manibanjang, a remote place in Darjeeling district in the state of West Bengal. While being in dilemma whether I should go there or not, I received a letter of appointment from Department of security to teach at Transit School with six month probation.

My transition from the beautiful red sandstone campus of Punjab University designed by Pierre Jeanerette under the guidance of Le Corbusier to the foothills of the Dhauladhar range with the gurgling river where the school for the adult refugee students from Tibet which prepared them in their transit to the life in exile was the most memorable and productive years of my life because this is where my eyes were opened to the reality of life. The work was not heavy and the time was abundant. By 2 in the afternoon, the classes would be over. So in the first year of service, I read voraciously. Every month, when I got the salary, I would pilgrim the book shops in McLeod Ganj and would bless myself with one of two books. In the second year, I started preparing for Fulbright Scholarship as well as M.A in Economics through Distance learning from Punjab University. My hard work paved my way to the interview for the scholarship, but did not get through it for criticizing the U.S foreign policy without knowing that the gatekeeper to my prospective university in the land of opportunity is the Uncle Sam. I planned to pursue M.A in four disciplines: Economics, English, History and Political Science. During my 3rd year, my parents asked me to take my younger brother along with me to Dharamsala as they were anxious that he would settle down with a Nepali girl. With the arrival of my younger brother, my daily routine changed though I completed my M.A without any flying colour due to the lack of strategic stroke in the exam. I applied for M.A in English from the Garwal University, because I was angry with Punjab University. But I gave it up as I had to spend time with my younger brother. As he played the guitar, he was in need of a drummer. So, I started learning the Octopad, an electronic drum, from a local Nepali. With a rudimentary drumming skill, we started jamming and writing songs with spontaneity.

Our first performance as a three piece band was at Miss Tibet contest at TIPA. Our band was called R-59. By then, I had joined Upper T.C.V School. Unlike the previous school, it was very hectic. Since I was by myself as my brother was employed and did not stay with me, I was free after class, so I continued learning the drums with the help of YouTube tutorials. During weekends, we would jam at his place in Gangchen Kyishong. And then he joined Upper T.C.V as an accountant. After a year or so, we applied for a family quarter and we got one where we jammed almost every night for an hour. We released our first and the only album during that period. By then, I had bought an acoustic drum set and had a fair command over the instrument. Our pala, after our mother's death, shifted to Dharmrasala to live with us.

Later my brother moved to live with his wife who had completed her 'amji' course and worked at MentseKhang. My bachelorhood of 4 years ended with the entry of Lobsang in my life in 2009.

And in 2010, I got selected for Fulbright Scholarship, but I was denied visa along with other 6 selected candidates on the pretext that many former scholars had not returned to India as per their bond and they further condescended that they don't want to waste the American taxpayers' money on us. That year, America was going through economic crisis. So, in 2011 I was jobless because I had to take leave for further studies and another teacher had already been appointed in my place to fill my absence.

Fortunately, I got the offer to work in T.C.V, Selakui, the elite school for Tibetan children, where I was by myself for a year during which I spent my time reading books leisurely and practicing the drums religiously. My colleagues would tease me what 'shabden' I did every afternoon and every day. I applied online for M.A English at IGNOU. I submitted my first assignment but I was informed that my admission would be cancelled if I did not pay my fees as a foreign student as I had not in my application stated my nationality as Indian. I tried to convince the director of the center that I am a Tibetan refugee residing in India. He assured me that the matter had to be discussed at the higher level. In the end, my admission was cancelled. Later I was told that I should have applied as an Indian and that no one would question me. I thought I paid the price for being honest. And then I got admission for the same degree at the Garwal University. However, I did not have enough time and energy to give justice to the course because I had realized due to my past experience that I had to prioritize relationships over dreams. Moreover, I was engrossed in my profession too. Even though I did not become a Fulbright, I choose to be a full bride, which was followed by fatherhood in 2015 which was the inception of the loss of personal freedom. After two years of Kunga's birth, we were blessed with a daughter on 2nd September, 2017. Since then, our life has been sandwiched between the professional and parental demands. I hardly got time to invoke the god through the drums. Instead our son started drumming the hell out of us. Nevertheless, my most fulfilling period of teaching experience of 20 years was the 7 years of service at the school. After I passed the litmus test of around three months by students, over the course of time I gained their trust and respect as I worked really hard to make their learning experiential, experimental, critical, sensible and self-directed mainly through project based pedagogy. After class I used to check their project work and work on my action research for two hours. During free periods, I used to research on the rubric to assess their project work and other activities to enhance their English language. During my stay there I progressed professionally to a great level.

Fortunately, our request for the transfer to Upper T.C.V was accepted in 2018, but new challenges were waiting for us. Kunga had turned 3 and Tselha was only 6 months old. Juggling between professional and parental responsibilities drained us because unlike former school older staff kids have no crèche facilities when they go to school. During brakes, they were on their own without any adults to monitor them from falling prey to the monkeys menace, stray dogs and the concrete play ground. So, I had to when the bell rang for the break run to the play ground to attend him. Five minutes before the lunch time, I would leave class and long jump the stairs to fetch him from his class to serve him lunch and then wait for the teacher to arrive to the class for the afternoon session of just half an hour. When his teacher comes after the bell goes, I sprint back to my indifferent class with the guilty huff of exhaustion for being late. After taking that period, I had to again rush back to collect my son whose classes are dismissed 45 minutes earlier than the rest of the school. In Monsoon, during lunch break, I and my son would lounge on the dirty sofa with his head on my lap in the rest room of the school kitchen staff him glued to the screen and me stuck to the novel. When our son reached stage 2, we had to overlook his safety but my mind was not free from the worry while at work. Moreover, I was at a saturation point of my career. I was in desperate need of a long break. So, in the end of 2019, I applied for a sabbatical which I was eligible for with a 15 year service to the institution. But the big but is that I was denied because two teachers from our section had already applied for it and they were granted the leave for they were senior to me. So, after much thinking, I took the risky step of resigning from the job. I had to.

I badly needed a break. I had to fulfill my dreams. And our daughter, Tselha, was ready to go to school.

And then, Pandemic struck us. India was under lockdown by the end of February 2020. We were stuck in our house sometimes for a week or so. However, we got to spend quality time with our kids. Lobsang took the responsibility to teach kids at home when she was free from teaching her.students online. I, being unemployed, took charge of the kitchen and teaching Kunga the drums in the evening after the screen time of two hours from 2:00 to 4:00 during which I studied M.A English, which did not started till August as I took admission in June session. So, I was not spending much time in preparing for M.A due to unavoidable constraints. Initially, I did not study at night, but later I had to as I was not able to complete the prescribed courses. Even though my initial plan had to be revised, it was worth spending time with kids. Kunga learned the basics of drumming. Tselha's personality opened up. She became more assertive, vocal and confident. Since I was not any pressure of my profession, I made the best use of my time doing certificate courses on smart phone ideography, guitar tones, ear-training, intermediate guitar master class and workshop on writing and publishing books. In addition, I learned Blues an hour every day except weekends. When the lockdown relaxed in the second year of Pandemic, every weekends we went for either tracking in the woods or picnic on meadows.

The final M.A exam I sat for was in December 2022 and by the end of March the result declared that I have mastered English literature with the first division.

The two years of being unemployed was the most productive period of my life. After 15 years of chasing my dream, I jolted it to reality.

CHAPTER EIGHT

Genla, You Are Not Always Right

In my dream, I heard something. I felt something on my head. It was Lobsang. Her face was lit up with the screen of her mobile phone. She was watching something. I felt irritated. With half closed eyes, I checked my mobile phone lying comfortably on the pillow against the wall. It was 4 AM. I am supposed to wake up at 6. I muttered my irritation. Losing my sleep, I too sought the company of my mobile phone. I don't remember when I fell asleep but the alarm set with the melody of nature jolted me up. With a heavy head, I rushed out of bed to the washroom. After attending to the nature's call and busy brushing and sparse facial splashes, I raced into my *bod-sok wonchuk*, *khen-cha*, cotton trowsers not *chuppa* and mountain boots not *sompa* to receive H.H.The Dalai Lama returning to Dharamsala from Ladakh.

I had to be at the school football ground at 7:30. There was only 10 minutes to go. I thought students and the staff would have already assembled and be ready to leave for McLeod Ganj by the ankle twisting short cut through the jungle. When I got there on time, the football ground was empty. I asked myself, "Am I late? Have they left?

Should I ride my scooter to get there on time?" During this interior monologue, I saw a female staff walking towards my direction from the other end of the ground. "Is she also late?" I comforted my alter ego. A male teacher walked down the stairs towards the ground. After some time, students started strolling down from their hostels. The head master also arrived with his lap top bag hanging on his tilted shoulder and started directing the students to stand in line and instructed us to take their attendance.

Instead of taking a sharp left turn from the ground towards the rocky short cut through the forest, we took the way down the school canteen by the homes and the laundry from where crossing across a short distance following the narrow path by Amala's mansion and her brother Kalurinpoche's labrang and further walking on the main road flanked by the forest, we reached McLeod. During this whole time, I preferred to be with the music on the earphones.

When we reached the main entrance to Tsukla Khang, we were told that we had to wait for at least two hours. So, standing near the welcoming decorated gate, I took out my mobile phone and continued reading a research paper from where I left off. Time passed easily. I read two research papers out of many on my phone.

Some restless students were hanging around instead of standing in line. The chairman of the Advisory Committee was persuading them to get back to line without any effect.

It started to drizzle and one of the organizers of the reception party asked me to cover the offering to His Holiness of roasted barley flour and whole wheat in an ornate wooden tray like container with my umbrella. So, I had to move to the other side of the gate where senior students were standing and one of them was sitting in a chair which was next to the table where the offering was placed. The organizer asked the boy to stand up and let me sit. I told the boy to keep sitting but he insisted me to sit. I sat on the chair raising the umbrella over the offering. There was murmur of His Holiness' cavalcade reaching Gangkyi. Everybody including who were loitering around became alert and the students who were hanging around stood beside me and the students who were huddled behind me were asked by the chairperson of Advisory Committee to stand in the front which was already crowded. Some students stood in front of me with their butts on my face while I was still sitting in the chair with my umbrella still hoisted but the frame is bent poking one of the students standing in front of my nose. He looked at me and my umbrella. I ignored him. He looked at me and my umbrella again with irritation. I ignored him. And he said to me, "Gen la, close the umbrella." "No, I will not," I responded curtly.

Expecting that His Holiness's cavalcade was nearing, squatting devout stood up including me. People were commenting that it is going to take longer to drive up from Gangkyi to Mcleaod with his followers on both sides of the road to welcome him and to steal his passing glance. While looking forward to His Holiness's arrival, standing beside the student, I remarked to him, "You don't have any common sense." "What do you mean?, he retorted. With a smirk , I said, " You don't seem to have any sense." What do you mean? You don't make any sense to me", said he with irritation. "Do I need to explain what I mean?", I asked. "Yes"

My response to his affirmation was a long silence. He said, "Gen la, you are not always right." "Yes, I agree. But what you did today was not right." He demanded what I meant. I reminded him that he stood in front of my face while I was sitting. He said, "Gen Karma Singey la instructed us to stand in the front. How can I defy his order as we are expected to follow the advice of the elders?" "Would you have climbed that tree if he asked you to do so?" asked I. He responded, " I am not a fool." "So, did he ask you to stand in front of me? You should have used your common sense to make the right judgment." He took a deep breath. His brows arched above his tensed eyes. He chose not to comment.

People got excited as they overheard the people on walki talkie communicating about the approach of His Holiness cavalcade. He chose to speak: You did not move because you did not want to lose the spot. I said to him, "Now, you are telling the truth. You stood in front of me to have a better audience of His Holiness. You thought that I stole your spot." I reminded him that I was asked by the organizer to move to the spot to cover the offering from rain with my umbrella." I assured him when His Holiness arrives I will move to another spot. I told him that he showed me his true color of his behavior. He said, " Are you going to pick on me in the class? Teachers often do that." " Is your work complete? Do you mind your own business?" asked I suggesting that he is not. With hesitation, he affirmed. I advised him not to worry and besides I don't have any time to harbor any ill feeling towards any one specially you.

People standing in line started jostling to get a better glimpse of His Holiness who arrives amidst swirling smoke of incense and peening of 'gyaling'. I quickly, as I assured the student, shifted to the other side of the gate. The organizer asked to hold one of the pots with the fake flowers to welcome His Holiness. My gaze drifted towards the student and he was looking at me. I smiled at him. His Holiness was nearing the gate slowly waving to his devotees. As he neared the gate, he decided to bless the offering. The door to his car was opened. The man with the offering moved towards him. Taking a pinch of the barley flour, he threw it in the air as an offering to the god and put the remaining in his mouth. I wondered the offering was out in open under the drizzle. Anyone could have adulterated it with an evil intention.

CHAPTER NINE

Your Are Fortunate

My heart pounded when a friend of mine called out to me, "Tenzin, the result is out." I felt a lump chocking my throat. I shouted back to her, "O.K. I am coming." I ran down the high cemented steps from my house to our math's teacher's place which was crowded with students like me who had appeared for Class X board exam in the month of March. I pushed my way through the crowd and stood over the math's teacher peering through his photo sensitive spectacles bending over the result sheet on his lap. I tried to find myself on the list of the name on the sheet, but it was a long and broad sheet. So, I shouted to him, "Sir, what are my marks?" He looked at me with irritation and scanned through the list with his index finger till my name and moved his finger further across the row and stopped at the marks I scored in his subject, which was Math. Without looking at me with a disappointed voice, he says, " 45." and points his finger at the row to copy the marks for the rest of the subjects. Without bothering to copy the marks of the rest of the subjects, with head hanging low I pushed my way out.

I climbed the steps back home. I sulked flat on my bed staring at the wall disbelieving that I got only 45 in Math. The images of me toiling through math problem for hours alone in the class many nights by candle light with the help of unreliable but dependable guide books flashed through my mind. My skeptical voice in my head said, "It is not possible. Go to the school and check it on the school notice board." Without wasting any time, I jumped out the bed and walked for more than an hour up and down the mountain to reach our school. Among the outdated notices cluttering the notice board was our fresh crispy result sheet. Again I felt a lump in my throat and my chest felt the beating of my nervous heart. I scanned for my name on the list with my index finger. There it was. My name. When transliterated correctly my first name means the protector of Buddha's teaching, but it is spelled in a similar fashion to the Sherpa conqueror of the Everest, Tenzing, which transliterates as the one who fights Buddha's teaching: Tenzing not Tenzin. Jokes apart, after I identified my name on the list, my vision blurred across the subjects which preceded Math. When my eyes caught the sight of Math, my vision focused on the score, but the number is deceptively the same:45. Past does not change. Present does. My alter ego, my inner voice, said to me, "You cannot pursue Science in Mussorie." I walked back home with the persistent and annoying thought in my head: I can't pursue Science in C.S.T, Mussorie.

Many years later while relearning Math for GRE preparing for Fulbright Scholarship, I had to face irritation and frustration of not my unreliable and dependable guide book, but my reliable and dependable guide, Mrs.Lobsang Dolma because I had to go back to basics to solve the complex mathematical problems. She could not believe that I did not know how to solve LCM. My pala who stayed with us in Upper T.C.V, feeling embarrassed to hear her shouting at me when I could not get through simple math concepts, told her privately that I did not listen to him when he told me to take math tuition like other students when I was facing class X board exam. He was true that I did not listen to him. The reason was that I did not want to burden him with additional expense because whenever I was home on holidays I often overheard him talking about how business was going down and prices were going up. Private tuition for math and science after class was a big business. Do you know why? These teachers did not teach in the class. I still have a vivid memory of our math teacher in dark glass and thick beard in Winter just walking around in the class with a shortened piece of chalk in his hand after a quick customary gesture of filling up the whole board with some sacred numbers and mysterious letters. We never thought of complaining because it was normal. Taking private tuition is a must. He did not teach us in the class because he taught at his home one batch of students in the morning before the school starts and two batches of students after school. It was not extra classes. It was private tuition for his extra personal profit.

And for your kind information, with the help of my reliable guide, Mrs.Lobsang Dolma, I got more than 50% in GRE math just in two months of preparation, which proves that I did not lack mathematical intelligence to get only 45 in math in the board exam provided I got a good teacher like her.

I did not do well in Science either even though it was not as bad as my performance in Math. We used to think that our Biology teacher was good because even though we did not understand what he was teaching from the textbook, he kept us busy copying answers to the textbooks questions from the black board. Our Physics teacher was an interesting character. Once I asked him out of curiosity how the paper prayer wheel turns with the help of butter lamp. I still remember that enlightening moment clearly. We were on the way down to my class in the senior block of the school building. Before answering to my query, he adjusted his Nepali cap on his head, held his thick glasses pressing his eyes to a meditative close to reflect. And then with a twinkling eyes and a broad grin, he answered with unfathomable confidence. Do you know what his answer was? He said, " I don't know. Go ask the scientists." I could not go to ask scientists, but I bought obscure science books for college students. One of them was Organic Chemistry. I don't know why I bought that book. It must be the title of the book that tempted me. I remember reading that book without any scientific comprehension. I was trying to decipher the content of the book with the language of literature. Recently, I heard that he retired after many years of his service as a Physics teacher in our school, where in the beginning when there were shortages of teachers in 1960s, it is said that he was a peon in the office. I hope after his retirement physical interactions and chemical reactions in the class in my Alma mater has progressed. Till I chose my stream to Arts after class X, I had never been to Science lab. We got marks for practical tests without being examined. Fortunately, I have not committed the crime of murdering any frogs or mice or shamelessly peered into the privacy of micro organisms through the microscope.

What about the computer lab? Yes, we have been there once. The experience was like entering a restricted holy shrine in some forbidden ancient temple. We were asked to remove our shoes. Those whose socks smelled, it was bare feet entry for them. When we got inside, we were instructed to kneel in front of a lonely device with thick screen fixed in a fat white plastic body with a protruding keyboard in the front on a high table. I thought It looked like a type writer from the future. We were not allowed to touch it. We were there for an audience with an incarnation of the 1st generation of personal computer. Did I learn computer? Yes, many years later after finishing college education when I started working. I learned to type on a broken borrowed laptop by typing a sentence which contained all the 26 letters of English language. I am still a computer illiterate.

Remembering our school library, I can still smell it. The musty odor which comes from the absence of human presence in a place for a long period of time like the dungeon of a palace buried under the ground unearthed after many centuries. The heavily sanitized smell in the air in the library was the chemical residue of some agents sprayed on the books to protect from the real book worms because there were no human books worms. I remember reading compiled comic books from the municipal library. I remember hunting second hand books shops during holidays, which was my favorite pass time.

The books I remember reading from the library were the books by P.G.Woodhouse. It was very difficult for my young mind to understand him. He was meant for adults. I remember reading something from a book I borrowed from the library. It was related to news reporting. The line from that piece that struck me was that news report should be careful of sensationalism. For example, instead of reporting Pakistan attacks India, the wording should be Pakistani Army attack Indian front. What I learned from that one line is we should avoid making sweeping statement over generalization. It is dangerous.

Are you curious to know about our P.T classes? My fleeting memories of P.T class of 12 years of stay in the school is being asked for the first time in my school life by the P.T master to run over the hurdles when I was in class X for the final assessment of my physical fitness when board exam was going on. So, these days whenever during Sports Day when I am a track judge for hurdles, my legs wobble, throat dries and heart throbs to see you, the athletes, sprint and spring over the hurdles to finish first.

If you ask me how my art class was, I hesitate to say that my mental canvas is blank. I don't see any memorable dashes and strokes except my drawing of fruits on a plate presented proudly on the wooden wall of our home where it stayed for many years. I can still see the defaced wall with the bad images of bat man and spider man which I drew when I was bored to death on weekends in my late Popo la's spider webbed home.

That's how the time passed and the class XII graduation day finally arrived. There was not any special function at school. We were just asked to assemble in the hall for some important announcement by the Rector. We were very curious as to what he has to tell us as school heads rarely spoke to us in person. Whenever they had to speak it was from an official distance during morning assembly. I haven't heard anger, frustration and inspiration in the speeches. It was just official. The reason why we were called to the assembly on our last day was to make some announcement relating to DOE scholarship and CTSA scholarships. We were informed that those who got distinction, i.e. above 75% will get scholarship from the Indian Government. That was my first and last career day of my school life. However, I was thrilled. I desperately wanted to get out of the town of Darjeeling to study in the metropolis. After convincing my father, together with my friend, for the first time I ventured out of Siliguri, which was the furthest place I had visited till then with a hazy dream and a clear sense of adventure. We landed in Delhi for college admission in the summer when the mercury recorded highest in the last decade. For somebody landing on the hot Indian plain from the cool mountain of the Queen of Hills, Darjeeling, the heat was maddening. It was so hot that the yellow brass locket which I was wearing burned my chest and turned greenish with salty sweat. So, before finding out colleges, we instinctively looked for a shelter. My friend, who had seen the world more than I did, suggested that we should try out at Youth Hostel for TCV students. I had no option but to follow him being awed by the sweltering heat and sprawling mess called Delhi. To our great relief, at the youth hostel office we were given accommodation for a nominal charge on the condition that we had to vacate the room if TCV students needed it. We had a great time looking into the sky lying on the rooftop at night to avoid the trapped heat in the room. There was water cooler to quench our thirsty throats. The food at the mess was nutritious and light on our shoe string budget. During day time, for the first time, I had to travel every day to look for colleges on crowded stinking rickety noisy hot big tin box on four wheels instead of my two legs which would take me wherever I wanted in the small town of Darjeeling. When we got off the bus, to navigate through the criss- cross of streets, we had to quarrel over the unfixed fare with the human engine which drove the tricycle with a plastic slippery narrow bench and a short roof over your bending necks. Three days passed applying for admission to various colleges without any hope of getting entry to any prestigious colleges because the cut off percentage remained above 95% which was out of our reach. During these times we noticed that TCV students were guided through the whole process of admission from supplying them with forms to filling them up to escorting them to the colleges. If we had not followed one of these escorts and TCV students from an un-intrusive distance trying unsuccessfully not to be noticed by them, we would have lost without direction. And finally after three days, the feared condition of the accommodation in the hostel fell on us. We were called to the office and instructed to leave in the afternoon because even though we were all Tibetan students, yet the preference was given to TCV students. We spent that afternoon with our rug sacks on our back looking for a cheap room on rent in the vicinity of the hostel. The cheapest rooms were very expensive for our financial status. The following night we stayed in a cheap room in M.T. watching MTV with swarming mosquitoes in a dizzying humidity. Ngawang Palden, who was not only my friend, but a guide and a companion to me as I was an alien in this part of the world, suggested at last being on the verge of pennilessness and shelterlessness that we should try out at Chandigarh. During this time, another reality struck me. As my shoe string budget was getting tighter and tighter I thought of the other source of income. I don't mean working part time. I was too immature to even think of that possibility. I mean the easy source of income: the CTSA scholarship. So, I went to the bureau, where the official revealed me the harsh reality. Can you guess what it was? Are you guessing that my scholarship was rejected? No, nothing of that sort. It was the shocking amount of the scholarship. It was shocking not because I hit the jack pot but because the amount was only 6000 rupees annually and in 5 days I had already spent 5000 rupees. At first I could not believe. So, I asked him to confirm if it was 6000 or 60000. He confirmed that figure with one zero less is the fact and the one with one more zero which I had added was my imagination. That day I realized the genius of the Indian mathematician who came up with the concept of zero. It is so powerful. More zeros in your bank balance can mean you are either a beggar or a billionaire.

Finally, we escaped to Chandigarh, the city beautiful. Yes its architectural design is beautiful. Since it is a planned city, it was less populated with humans, homes and garbage. Chandigarh was the antonym of Delhi. I instantly fell in love with the city.

In the end, we settled in this beautiful city. What happened after that is another story.

The reason why I have told you this particular chapter of the story of my life is that compared to other Tibetan students like me in CSTs, you, the students in TCVs, and specially you, in TCV,Selaqui, are fortunate.

You know that you are fortunate because you are often told so, but I have been trying to show you how fortunate you are because even though I am now part of a TCV family, being an outsider I can see things which you cannot see because you take them for granted.

For example,

You have a very dedicated teaching and non teaching staff, who, most of them are ex-TCVians, which I think is the main reason why the standard of education in TCV is comparatively better than other Tibetan Schools because they have affinity with their alma-mata. They came to the school to learn and have come back to serve.

TCV administration prioritizes you over its staff. That's why if you look at the percentage of salary in the overall budget allocation of our school, it is only 24% whereas in other schools the big chunk of the budget is gobbled by the payment of salary to their staff. Even in the poorest schools run by Indian Governments, the staffs are rich.

The discussion in TCV schools among educators is not whether teachers teach in the class or not but rather the discussion is on how to teach effectively to raise the existing standard to a higher level. The effort is to enrich your learning experience on all fronts. For instance, private tuition is banned in TCV schools. Instead you are provided personal tuitions by teachers voluntarily or the school organizes remedial classes for you if you don't do well in tests. It happens only in TCV Schools.

There is no question of math teacher not teaching in the class as it was in my case. Rather they over teach you because many a times I have had the experience of waiting outside the class for the science and math teachers to leave so that I can take my class. I have witnessed teachers quarreling over the repeated theft of one another's teaching time and space. This is because we are willing to teach you if you have the willingness. But when a teacher centers his talk during morning assembly around the theme, 'You are the master of yourself' and when the head of the institution reiterates in his passionate talks the same theme, but in a different wordings, which is, 'You are the architect of your own destiny', what it indicates is that you are not making the best use of your time and resources available to you.

You know that you are fortunate but you have not realized it. Realization comes through action. So, please put all your effort to grow and improve yourselves.

By the way I have not told you about my music class in school. Do you know I can play the dramnyen? Should I play a piece for you? But I don't need this piece of instrument. I can play without it. Do you know how? This is how. Listen...Tang Taring Tang Taring Taring Taring Tang Tang Tang Taring Taring Taring.... So, can I play the dramnyan? You may so no, but this is how we have been taught to play the instrument without touching it in the music class in my school.

You are fortunate...Taring Taring Tang...Wo....Ya..la...you are fortunate. Remember that.....Taring Taring Tang.....

CHAPTER TEN

Can Artificial Intelligence and Human Intelligence Co-exist?

Is science fiction a mere figment of imagination? Or is it an imaginative prediction of future based on the scientific trend from the past to the present?

Well, I affirm with the latter. What about you? Is it just a flight of imagination? Or is it a calculated prediction?

Now, let me share the premise of a science fiction movie I watched recently on Netflix entitled Atlas in which an AI robot meant to help a human family goes rogue and becomes a terrorist leader of AI threatening to wipe out humanity from the face of the earth to usher in an era dominated by AI beings. Isn't scary? Is it possible? Probably not but not impossible considering the pace at which AI is developing. Even though it is at its nascent stage at present, its generative capability is demonstrated in the function of Chat GPT. There is a high probability of its misuse by the vested interest which could cause existential threat to humans. I am not just raising this concern for the sake of argument but I am voicing the similar lines of the experts which I would like to quote:

1. Stephen Hawking: The renowned physicist warned that AI could be the "worst event in the history of our civilization" unless its development is strictly and ethically controlled. He feared that AI could potentially surpass human intelligence, leading to unintended consequences.

2. Elon Musk: The CEO of Tesla and SpaceX has repeatedly sounded alarms about AI, calling it the "biggest existential threat" to humanity. He has advocated for proactive regulation to ensure AI development is aligned with human values and safety.

3. Nick Bostrom: The philosopher and AI theorist argues in his book "Superintelligence: Paths, Dangers, Strategies" that advanced AI could pose a significant threat if its goals do not align with human welfare. He stresses the need for robust strategies to manage and mitigate these risks.

First and foremost, AI can threaten the existence of humanity:

Because of the rapid advancement of computer technology and generative capacity of AI, it will surpass human intelligence. More than 20 years ago on May 11,1997, a rudimentary AI powered computer program called Deep Blue beat the human counterpart in the game of chess. He was the reigning World Chess Champion Garry Kasparov. So, we can imagine how far AI has developed since then and how far it can advance in future. AI can go out of our control and instead of solving our complex problems, they can be the cause of existential threat to humanity as the eminent scientists like Stephen Hawkings and the influential personalities like Elon Musk have expressed their concern about the potential danger of AI to humanity.

Furthermore, AI can disrupt the basic fabric of our economic and social system:

For our generation it is normal for us to hear the automated voice responding to our query relating to some services. Humans from their jobs are displaced by machines. Millions have lost their jobs and more are losing or are at the risk of losing their livelihoods because AI enhanced robotics are more efficient and cost effective. Such a scenario will lead to economic inequality which could cause social upheaval. Not only the low skilled workers will be affected but also highly skilled professionals like doctors and engineers will be replaced by AI machines.

In addition to economic disruption, AI can disturb our long standing ethical and moral values:

For better efficiency and cost effectiveness, our lives will be more dependent on AI. We will make decisions based on AI. What would be role of our elders who are the guardians of our culture if AI become our guide and mentor? You must have heard of the self-driving car. In case of an accident in such a car providing taxi service, who is responsible? The car without the human driver or the service provider or the manufacturer? Another chilling scenario is the development of autonomous weapons which means that without human intervention machines will make decisions relating to life and death. Can we fully trust AI algorithms to run our life as the system learns from data we feed them which could be biased? People are hired and fired with the help of AI system. Law enforcement agencies are resorting to AI to solve criminal cases.

AI invades our privacy:

Are the services provided by Facebook and Instagram free of cost? Is the information collected for you at the tip of your finger by Google free of cost? Yes, you don't have to pay any monetary fees but you are selling your privacy to these corporations because they monitor your activities on these social media and are privy to your likes and dislikes about people, places and products. They sell your private life to the multinational companies to sell their products through their nagging and invasive advertisements.

Lastly, AI will outpace us to regulate and control it effectively:

AI can sing in your voice even if you are tone deaf. AI can write a novel for you even if you haven't written a single page in your life. AI can even paint. AI is developing at an alarming pace based on the ever-growing data on the internet. So, timely regulation is a huge challenge. Moreover, the development of AI is driven by profit motive of the big corporations rather than human welfare. Governments can use it to control their citizens with misinformation and surveillance. So, these two entities may not be interested to control and regulate AI fully for their own vested interest even if they could.

In the end, who is going to benefit from the development of AI? Not the whole humanity as suggested by its proponents, but a small elite section of humanity: only the rich and the powerful. If we flip back the pages of history, it is replete with the accounts of the rich and the powerful exploiting the technological development to their advantage.

For example, during stone age, when humans learned to make crude tools out of stones, we dominated the animal kingdom. We hunted them for food and cloth and wiped out the woolly mammoths. As we advanced to the iron age, with new weapons, kings expanded their empire with the force of their army killing millions of innocent people.

With the industrial revolution, the companies and their kings started colonizing other countries to expand their market and for resources. Now, we are in the cusp of information revolution, it has definitely democratized the access to knowledge for common people, but the rich and the powerful, viz, the corporates and the governments, have used them to mislead the people with their tempting advertisements and false information for their vested interest.

Presently, the new era of AI is unfolding with awe inspiring possibilities to enhance human life which our worthy opponents have enumerated at great length. However, it is human predicament that our egocentric nature has caused a lot of destruction. The advancement of science has not only improved the quality of life, but with the production of weapons of mass destruction we have jeopardized the very existence of life on earth. Should I remind you of the nuclear holocaust in Japan when lethal weapon was dropped on Hiroshima and Nagasaki at the end of the W.W II?

Nuclear weapons don't have any intelligence of its own. It is being regulated and controlled by the governments. But what about AI which is self-generating and deep learning which can be misused by the rich and powerful for their own vested interest of profit making and power mongering which could result in.

CHAPTER ELEVEN

Is AI A Threat To Human Employment?

Let me start by telling you a story. It is about Raghu. He used to own a cybercafé 15 years ago when he was in late 20s. He had a thriving business. You had to wait for turn to surf the internet specially on weekends and evenings when all his bulky desktop computers would be occupied by his customers. And then when Steve Job created the unnecessary need for a device which we did not need called smart phones and the internet became cheaper in India because of Mukesh Ambani's capitalist compassion, Raghu's computers started collecting dust rather than money for him. As a result, he started dealing with cables, adapters, phone covers, earphones and so on. His primary business was phone recharge. But these days, you can charge on your own. You don't need him. Now a days he is selling vegetables. He is in late 40s. He has family to support now.

So, what is the theme of the story? Adaptation? Resilience? Resourcefulness?

Yes, all of them. Because of his resilience and resourcefulness, he has adapted to the threat to his employment caused by technological advancement, specifically information technology in his case.

My worthy opponent's one and only singular solid main meaty argument against the motion, most probably, would be that people will lose jobs due to advancement in AI, but more jobs will be created by AI. If they say so, I could not agree more with them. With the advancement of any kind of new technology, old jobs will be replaced by new jobs.

Therefore, I am not going to rebut my opponents' core argument, rather defend my stand that whether AI will create new opportunities of employment or not, the threat to human employment remains in the real present, the immediate future and the distant future. However, the survival instinct of humans will overcome any threat to our existence not just our means of livelihood.

Now, let me support my basic argument with some hard data:

In the last two decades, since 2000, 1.7 million people have lost their jobs in manufacturing industries as a result of increased competition and lower wages due to automation.

In the recent past, according to Resume Builder Survey, ChatGPT has replaced workers in 23.5% of U.S companies.

And it is predicted by Goldman Sachivia and BBC that 300 million jobs which is 9.1% of jobs world wide will be affected by AI. By 2030, 14% of employees which is 375 million workers will be forced to change their career.

Are all jobs threated by AI? No. According to IMF, 40% of jobs worldwide are vulnerable to AI because in emerging economy, millions of people lack access to internet. Therefore, the threat of AI automation increases with the advancement of their economy. Whereas in advanced economies 60% of jobs will be impacted by AI as the companies will rely heavily on automation for efficiency and cost effectiveness.

Who are most vulnerable to AI's threat to employment? As per the findings of Golman Sachs, 25% of all work tasks will be affected by AI. Out of which, AI will take over 46% of administrative role, 44% of legal jobs, 6% of construction work and 4% of maintenance jobs.

Next, what is the relationship between your employability and educational level in the world dominated by AI?

PEW reports that only 3% with a high school degree, 12% with high school diploma, 19% with college experience and 27% with at least Bachelors Degree will face the danger of losing their jobs because of AI.

In conclusion, I reiterate that my main argument that the threat to human employment will always be there with the advancement of any new technology including Artificial Intelligence, but the human spirit of resilience and adaptation will overcome any kind of threat. The history of human evolution is the testament of it.

So, if you hate to adapt and avoid the threat of AI to your employability, as the data suggest, don't go to school. Don't go to college. The more educated you are, the more chance of your job being taken by AI. At present and in the near future, the people with job security are construction workers, plumbers, electricians, nannies, waiters, cooks.........and......beggars.

But jokes apart, we cannot deny the fact that the threat of AI to human employment is clear and present.

CHAPTER TWELVE

Competition In Schools Hampers The Holistic Development of Students

(Proposition)

Dr. Benjamin S. Bloom, a pioneer in educational psychology, showed that competition, when used as a motivational tool, can significantly enhance student achievement. His work on Bloom's Taxonomy of Educational Objectives emphasizes the importance of intellectual competition in cognitive development.

From an evolutionary standpoint, competition has played a significant role in the survival and reproduction of our species. Natural selection has favored individuals who were competitive in securing resources, finding mates, and protecting their offspring. This drive for competition can be considered an inherent aspect of our evolutionary history.

Firstly, competition instils crucial life skills

Our schools mirror the real world where to be successful we need problem solving skills, adaptability and the ability to perform under pressures to the challenges of disruptions caused by the unprecedented advancement of technology. Competitions teach us to set goal, work diligently and overcome obstacles which are essential for the holistic development of students.

Secondly, competition can serve as a powerful motivator. As competition drives us to set goals and work hard to pursue excellence, it builds our character like discipline, perseverance and determination.

Thirdly, competition encourages innovation and excellence. In a competitive environment, students strive to reach their full potential. They are encouraged to push boundaries which help them to reach new standards of achievement because they are more likely to explore their interests and talents. Students excel in the areas they are passionate about which foster their creativity to reach higher levels of achievements.

Fourthly, competition can lead to a strong sense of self-esteem and accomplishment. As students become goal oriented, diligent, and disciplined and driven to excel in their chosen field, they are more likely to succeed as a result of which they gain confidence which impacts various aspects of their life. They develop a strong sense of self-growth.

Fifthly, competition provides the opportunity to discover our strengths and weaknesses. It helps us to discover our strengths and weaknesses by identifying the areas where we can excel and the areas we need to improvement which is the basis for a well-rounded individuals.

Lastly, competition can enhance social and emotional development. Competition is a great teacher who guides us how to handle success and failure gracefully. Through competition, we learn the importance of sportsmanship, teamwork and respect for others which are vital life skills which go beyond the academic knowledge which are essential of our holistic development.

In the end, if my worthy proponents argue that competition can lead to stress and anxiety in students, I, despite being the opponent, fully support them. However, it is essential to remember that competition itself is not the cause of stress; it depends upon how it is managed and how the pressure of expectations is put on us. So, what we need in schools is creating a balanced competitive environment where students are motivated to excel while also providing them with the necessary support and resources to deal with stress.

Moreover, competition doesn't have to be only about defeating others. It can be about self-improvement and personal growth as students can be taught to compete against themselves and to strive to do better, which can be as effective in promoting holistic development.

Therefore, let us support an education system that adopts competition as an engine to drive our students in their journey to be well-rounded, resilient, and successful individuals.

Last but not the lest, let me assure you that competition in schools, when properly managed, is an asset, not a liability, in the pursuit of the holistic development of students.

(Opposition)

"Sudhanshu Pandey didn't look the kind of teenager who would succumb to depression. Tall and well-built with hair that was always gelled, the 17-year-old was known to his friends as a cheerful, happy-go-lucky sort of guy. A student of Class XI at DPS-Noida, he was weak in his studies and barely managed to pass in his chosen subject. But if he was bothered he didn't show it to his friends.

On March 4, the day the Class XI results were to be announced, Sudhanshu seemed unusually reluctant to go to school. He told his mother to walk to the bus stop with his younger brother, promising her that he would follow them in a couple of minutes. But when his mother came back, she found his room locked from inside. When they broke open the door, his parents found that Sudhanshu had hanged himself to death from the ceiling fan using his mother's sari.

They found a suicide note on his bed in which he wrote: "Bye everybody. I'm committing suicide. Nobody else is involved. I have decided to end my life because the pressure has started to get to me and I cannot take it any longer. I love my family and I hope they will understand. I love my brother Siddharth and I would like to wish him all the best for the future... I hate the Eco teacher but I'm not doing this because of her.""

What I have just narrated is not a fiction but a fact. It is an extract from a news article written by Raj Chengappa on India Today.

So, why did he commit suicide? Can you tell me?

To begin with, the excessive competition has a negative effect on our mental and emotional health because the emphasis on academic excellence measured only by grades and scores puts enormous pressure on us. Failure in exams is equalled to failure in life. Not only the school but also the parents exert unnecessary pressure on us to be always on the top. When students can bear the pain of climbing

Achilles hill, they jump off to relieve themselves of the dreadful pain.

Moreover, the rat race competitive environment hinders the advancement of our social and creative skills. In such an environment, as we try to outperform our peers to cross the finishing line, we become self-centred. We don't value cooperation. We lose our sense of empathy. The 21st century requires us to be interdependent to be successful. We have to, through collaboration, find creative solutions to the challenges thrown at us by the ever changing environment because of the rapid technological advancement.

Furthermore, the toxic atmosphere of competition feeds immoral practices among us. Our relentless pursuit of success in academic field has led to academic dishonesty like cheating in the exam, plagiarism in write ups, copying notes from others without one's effort and so on. This lack of integrity can have a far reaching consequence for the society, which is reeling under corruptions.

In addition, the competition in capitalist system, which our schools are part of, rewards only material progress rather than our spiritual growth. Categorizing students into different classes in schools based only on their academic records is basically meant to prepare students to be the faithful and obedient workers in the offices and factories of the capitalist empire, which with their tools of mass media like televisions, newspapers and magazines in olden days and now- a- days, social media like Facebook, Instagram and other digital platforms, control our mind to believe that being successful means owing Mercedes, vacationing in Maldives, shopping in Malls and living in Taj Mahals like maharajas. So, while chasing the vicious material success, our life ends without having time to open the door of spirituality.

Finally, in contrary to competition, an educational environment that prioritizes cooperation over competition nurtures holistic development. When students are encouraged to collaborate, they learn the importance of teamwork and cooperation. They develop empathy and a sense of social responsibility, which are vital for becoming well-rounded individuals who contribute positively to society.

Furthermore, the emphasis on holistic development encourages students to explore a wide range of interests and passions. This exploration can lead to the discovery of talents and passions they might not have otherwise realized. It promotes creativity and innovation, which are essential for solving the complex problems of our rapidly changing world.

However, unfortunately, we live in a world where we are in a rat race to outdo others. We are under constant pressure to outperform our peers academically, athletically and socially because our worth is measured in terms of our achievements in the exam hall, on the track and field and in the social circle.

So, we must take a break and introspect and ask: What is the cost of this competition? Aren't we being denied the true purpose of education, which is the holistic development consisting of not only academic excellence but also emotional, social, moral and spiritual growth?

Let us get rid of the competition in schools so that the impersonal horrifying news headline like "Every hour, one student commits suicide in India" does not appear again.

CHAPTER THIRTEEN

Wish Fulfilling Gem

In the utter darkness of our recent history, a gem was found in Taktser, Eastern Tibet on 6th July, 1935. The gem occupied, in 1950, the vacant golden throne emitting the rays of hope. The gem was then not 16 million years old. The gem was merely 16 years old. The gem was our compassionate leader,Jetsun Jamphel Ngawang Lobsang Yeshe Tenzin Gyatso, His Holiness the 14th Dalai Lama. Since this gem was the only twinkling hope in the darkness overcastted by the Red Ants of Communist China in Tibet, it was decided after human and divine deliberation that the gem should not be in the greedy hands of the Communist Government.

So, followed by around 80,000 devotees, he, after a long hostile Himalayan journey hiding from the fuming Red Dragon, our snow lions, took refuge under the blazing sun of India.

What happens next is well known to all of you. The rest as they say is history, but it is not over. The history is in making. He is still writing our history and that of the world.

Only the gem like eyes could have the farsightedness of the vision for our fight for our cause. As you know, with the help of Nehru, he set up schools for Tibetan children and settlements for Tibetan people to preserve our history, culture and religion.

The reason why our struggle outshines the misleading propaganda of Chinese government is because of his visionary transplantation of Tibetan roots in a foreign soil. Look at me. I am standing wearing Tibetan dress in front of you representing my school speaking in English with my Tibetan tongue and Tibetan mindset to convince you that H.H. The Dalai Lama is not only the Gem of Tibet but also of the world. How has this been possible for me and thousands of others like me in the past and thousands to come in future? It is only because of his greatness and kindness. By the way, who is Dr.Lobsang Sangay? Our Sikyong, isn't it? But, before he went to Harvard University, he had been to a Tibetan Refuge School for 12 years eating black coarse tingmos and watery stews with occasional animal proteins of eggs and meat studying with bare minimum facilities and faculties.

TIPA, Tibetan Institue of Performing Arts, founded by H.H.The Dalai Lama in August, 1959, has been in the forefront of preserving and promoting authentic Tibetan traditional music and dance from different regions of Tibet. The teachers trained in this institute are teachers in our schools playing a very vital role in passing on the unique art to the Tibetan children. In schools, these professionally trained teachers impart the knowledge and skill of playing traditional instruments like Tibetan lute, flute, yanghen, piwang and drums. Students are taught folk songs and dances in sync with our rich cultural heritage.

The three seats of learning, Sera, Gaden and Drepung, though its spirit and foundation in Tibet destroyed by Communist China, have found a strong base in South India, where Tibetan Buddhism is flourishing and spreading their roots to different parts of the world including Buddhist

China. Every year, thousands of Doctorates of Buddhist Philosophy graduate from these spiritual universities upholding the ancient flame of wisdom.

On my last visit to a settlement in South India, I was invited to a wedding ceremony. I was surprised to witness the traditional beauty of the wedding. I was told that the ceremony they carried out has been continued for thousands of years. I had not had such an experience at a Tibetan wedding earlier because I did not live in a Tibetan settlement. I was alien to our own culture. I thought what if we had scattered all over India. What if we had no settlements-our own tiny islands in India? We would be swept away with the mainstream multi cultures of India and multinational multibillion corporations of the globalized world. According to www.centraltibeanreliefcommittee.org, there are 58 Tibetan settlements in India, Nepal and Bhutan. They are like the living museum of Tibet preserving our culture and tradition as the real Tibet is dying a slow death in the hands of hungry Han leaders.

In exile, to prepare for a democratic future in Tibet, he established Central Tibetan Administration based on democratic principles. Starting with Kalon Tripa appointed directly by His Holiness The Dalai Lama till 1990, when the 10th Assembly of Tibetan People's Deputies was dissolved for the election of the members of the assembly , now there are 46 members in the Assembly of Tibetan People's Deputies with Sikyong who is directly elected by the people. The post of Sikyong was entrusted with all the remaining temporal power of H.H.The Dalia Lama on 29th May 2011 ending the 368 year old tradition of the Dalai Lamas being both spiritual and temporal head of Tibet. It is a true example of statesman. Who else in the political history of any country has relinquished his authority on his own to his people? None for the benevolent reason which H.H.The Dalai Lama has.

In 1989, H.H.The Dalai Lama was awarded Nobel Peace Prize. This is what Egil Aarvik, Chairman of The Norwegian Nobel Committee said in the end in his presentation speech, "In awarding the Peace Prize to H.H. the Dalai Lama we affirm our unstinting support for his work for peace, and for the unarmed masses on the march in many lands for liberty, peace and human dignity." For the last 50 years, he has been travelling extensively around the world, more than 67 countries spanning 6 continents, meeting powerful leaders and powerless people to share the power of compassion. He has initiated dialogues with religious heads of different faiths to promote interfaith religious harmony. Since 1980s, he has been interacting with world renowned scientists in the field of neuroscience and psychology to understand the intricate workings of mind to help people achieve a peace of mind. With his humility and humor, he has won the heart of millions including some Hollywood and Bollywood stars.

He has received more than 150 awards. He has been honored with honorary doctorates by various universities. He has authored and co-authored 110 books. Among them, Beyond Religion: Ethics for a Whole World, The Art of Happiness: A Handbook for Living Ethics for a New Millennium and, The Universe in a Single Atom: The Convergence of Science and Spirituality are some of his best sellers. He has been the champion of secular ethics which are incorporated in curriculum in universities and schools abroad.

When I came across his three commitments which I have noticed he reiterates often, I was a little bit disappointed. His three commitments are: firstly, the promotion of basic human values or secular ethics in the interest of human happiness; secondly, the fostering of inter-religious harmony and thirdly; the preservation of Tibet's Buddhist culture, a culture of peace and non-violence.

Why is his commitment towards Tibet at the last? Should not his priority be us? Is not he *our* leader?

But I was wrong, he is not only the wish-fulfilling gem of Tibet but also of the whole world. In the world which is divided by boundaries on narrow lines of communalism, regionalism, nationalism, sectarianism, religionism, he has gone beyond them walking and talking for humanism. After all, he is the manifestations of Avalokiteshavara or Cherenzig, the Bodhisattva of Compassion, the enlightened being who has postponed his own nirvana and chosen to take rebirth to serve humanity.

CHAPTER FOURTEEN

Should Dalai Lama Wear 'tika' And Skull Cap?

In the Queen of Hills, Darjeeling, on the first day of Losar, we would visit 'gangchen', a mountain top, where both Hindu bells and Buddhist drums sing in harmony, where the prayer flags of both the religious communities dance to the purity of the crisp wind. After offering our prayers, down the hill, along the road side, there are pundits who are keen to bless you with 'tika', which I liked to have one on my forehead between my eyes as I thought it looked cool like the don in Mumbai gangster movies. But, pala would not allow me because he would reason that the red paste they smear on their forehead symbolize blood of an animal sacrifice, which is prohibited in our religion. Anyways, I usually had one when I hung out with my friends in'gangchen' and would wipe it off before returning home.

So, when I saw His Holiness the Dalai Lama with the' third red eye' with a glowing smile in news papers greeted by the saffron clad priests, my narcissistic sense of humour allowed me to quip that he was a rebel like me. Later I saw him donning the skull cap in mosques and synagoguesand covering his head with a cloth in gurudwarasaccompanied by the bearded religious authorities. I have also seen him murmuring prayers in his meditative eyes with his heart shaped hands in front of the crucified Christ flanked by hiscrusaders who are committed to crush poverty.

Why there is an urgent need for the promotion of religious harmony?

What do these images of him prove of him? Why does he mingle with the pundits, the imams and the priests? Is it for the cause of six-million Tibetans in chains? No, it is for the greater humanity. Because,even though we ignore it, history has taught us that we have caused immense suffering to one another in the name of religion as J.Krishnamurthi, the great philosopher, said that no institutions have caused more suffering to mankind than the organized religions.

Scientists have found through the anthropological examination of many Mexican archaeological sites that the religious conflict has been dividing human society for more than 2,000 years which is contrary to the belief that religion acted as a unifying force of societies in the early state.Even if,according toEncyclopedia of Wars authored by Charles Phillips and Alan Axelrod, only 123 out of 1763 documented records of warsfought have been incited by religious cases, yet the Crusades killed nearly one to three million people, and the Inquisition left about 3000 people death.

And in the recent history religious intolerance has been on the rise resulting in death and destruction. For example,According to Pew, in 2018 more than a quarter of the world's countries experienced a high incidence of hostilities motivated by religious hatred, mob violence related to religion, terrorism, and harassment of women for violating religious codes.

The surge in religious violence is aglobal phenomenon affecting every religious group. A 2018 Minority Rights Group report shows that mass killings and other forms of atrocities are have been increasing in countries irrespective of whether they are affected by war or not. The minorities in Syria, Iraq, Nigeria, India, Myanmar, Pakistan and Bangladesh have been the victims of brutal hostilities while Muslims and Jews have suffered increasing hostilities acrossEurope.Hindus have experienced religious animosity in more than 18 countries. The governments in 55 countries out of 198 countries of the world put heavy restrictions on religions, particularly in Turkey, Egypt, Russia, India and Indonesia.

RELAC data indicates that since 1975, there has been steady rise in the number of armed conflicts worldwide relating to religious issue conflicts whereas there has been declining trend in terms of number of armed conflicts caused by non-religious conflicts.

What does H.H.The Dalai Lama's Commitment to Religious Harmony Mean?

Therefore, H.H the 14th Dalai Lama has been crusading for global peace and harmony with his three main commitments, as stated on www.tibetmusium.org., viz.,

"1. As a human being,finding ways to promote human values such as compassion, forgiveness, tolerance, contentment and self discipline. All human beings are the same, we all want to gain happiness and avoid suffering. Even those who do not believe in religion recognize the importance of human values as a source of happiness in their lives. His Holiness the Dalai Lama refers to these human values as secular ethics.

2. As a religious practitioner, finding ways to promote religious harmony and understanding among the major religious traditions of the world. There are ideological and philosophical differences among religious traditions, but they all have the same potential to create good human being. It is therefore important for all religious traditions to respect one another and recognize the value of each other's respective tradition. One truth and one religion are relevant on an individual level. But, for the community at large, several truths, several religions are necessary.

3. As a Tibetan holding the title of the Dalai Lama, who is fully trusted by Tibetan people both within and outside Tibet, the third commitment is to endeavor to preserve the Buddhist culture, to strive for Tibet's cause and to assume the role of an independent spokesperson of Tibetan people living under oppression out of which the promotion of religious harmony is the key to end the suffering caused by religious intolerance."

So, what inference we can draw from the statement of his commitment to promote religious harmony and understanding among major religious traditions of the world is that he doesn't believe in religious fundamentalism but values the diversity of religious traditions with the potential to benefit the society. Because of which he advocates that all the religious traditions should respect one another irrespective of differences in ideology and philosophy as every religion encourages us to practice 'love, compassion, forgiveness and self-discipline'. To put it in H.H The Dalai Lama's words, "In short, since all major traditions have the same practice, just different methods and different philosophies, but with the same purpose, that is the ground for mutual respect."

Moreover, he argues that we should celebrate diversity of religions because they cater to the different dispositions of people. Hence, he does not favour the coerced conversion of a person to a different religion as he advises, "It is better to keep one's own religious tradition. In Mongolia, missionaries pay people $15 to convert to Christianity. So some people go to them and convert each year, over and again, just to collect $15 each time! I advise these missionaries not to interfere and to let people there stay traditional Buddhists. This is the same as when I tell Western people to keep their own religions.The best is to have more information. This helps to develop respect. Therefore, keep your Christian tradition, if you are Christian, but gain understanding and knowledge of other traditions."

In his address to the inter-faith seminar organised by the International Association for Religious Freedom, LadakhGroup, in Leh on 25 August 2005, he reasons that all the conflicts are man-made born by our distorted minds and every religion provides solution to control our mind but if we are biased towards our own religion we cannot see the reality. Therefore, in order to resolve a conflict, both sides, being sensitive to each other's issues, should engage in dialogue. He emphasizes, "Suspicion of each other will only harm both communities. Therefore, it is very important to live in harmony and analyse where the opinion of the other lies. The best way to do this is to engage in dialogue, dialogue and dialogue."

H.H.The Dalai Lama believes that the basis for the promotion of religious harmony is mutual respect for different religious traditions because of the similarity of their common values and principles; and by being open to learn and understand each other's traditions through close contact which can enrich one's own tradition.

What does he propose to Promote Religious Harmony?

In his book, entitled,Towards True Kinship of Faiths: How the World's Religions Can Come Together, he elaborates four types of interreligious dialogue to achieve the goal of religious harmony: (1) dialogue among scholars of religions at the academic level, which focuses on doctrinal similarities and differences with emphasis on the purpose of religions; (2) dialogue among genuine spiritual practitioners about deep religious experiences; (3) dialogue among leaders of religions to speak and pray from one common platform; (4) joint participation in pilgrimages to holy sites and rites of other religions.

What is evident from the news reports on his inter-faith dialogues is that the most prominent inter religious dialogues he has been engaged out of the four types are the dialogues among leaders of religions to speak and pray from one common platform and the joint participation in pilgrimages to holy sites and rites of other religions. My limited online research on the 1st and 2nd types of interreligious dialogues have not led mefind his effort on those fronts. I believe these two areas of dialogues are more challenging than the latter two because the ultimate purpose of the world religions and the paths to get there are different. If His Holiness, in his lifetime, can bring some changes in that direction and if not then, other religious leaders, in future, can lead in that direction; it would be a great service to the humanity.

What is the global response to his commitment?

In recognition of his commitment, he has been invited to various inter-faith dialogues, for instance, the Photo gallery, under the category: interfaith-dialogue, on www.dalailama.com, shows that since 2009 to 2019 His Holiness had been attended around 24 inter-faith dialogues in India and abroad. During his international travels, he has met, in addition to political leaders, many religious heads and leaders. He has met Pope Paul VI, Pope John Paul II, Pope Benedict XVI, and the Archbishop of Canterbury, Dr. Robert Runcie as well as the leaders of Eastern Orthodox Christianity, Islam, Hinduism, Judaism, and Sikhism.

The Dalai Lama is a member of the Board of World Religious Leaders as part of The Elijah Interfaith Institute. He took part in the Third Meeting of the Board of World Religious Leaders in Amritsar, India, on 26 November 2007 to deliberate on the topic; Love and Forgiveness. He inaugurated "World Religions-Dialogue and Symphony" conference in Gujarat in 2009. In 2010, the Dalai Lama launched the Common Ground Project in Bloomington, Indiana, U.S.A. The Dalai Lama and Prince Ghazi bin Muhammad of Jordan had planned the project which is based on the book Common Ground between Islam and Buddhism.

He has been hailed for his effort to achieve his ideal. In his praise, speaking at theKhadotYarchosChenmo festival, SonamWangchuk, award-winning innovator and education reformist said,"At a time when the world is divided and going away from one another. At a time when even in Ladakh, various sects of even the same religion were going apart from each other, different sects having differences and distances, your message of harmony and togetherness is doing magic,"

But he has been criticized for just talking and doing nothing much about it as skeptics argue that there has not been much change in reality. In addition, critics have cast doubts over his pluralism because they point that the basis of his ideal to promote religious harmony is exclusively entrenched in Buddhist philosophy whereby he believes that the ultimate truth, i.e, salvation, can be achieved only through Buddha's path. His inclusiveness and respect for other religions in his pursuit for the promotion of religious harmony hinges on the similarity of universal values of all the religious traditions like love, compassion, forbearance, discipline, and so on. On a philosophical and doctrinal level, he has been suspected of not looking upon other religions as equal. Jane Compson, in his essay, "The Dalai Lama and the world religions: a false friend?" makes a scathing concluding remark, "In a pluralist approach, tolerance is achieved through relinquishing the exclusivity or ultimacy of the teachings of any one particular religious tradition. In contrast, the Dalai Lama's acceptance of other religions is enabled precisely by his adherence to the teachings of dGe Lugs Buddhism as ultimate."

People who criticize him for not bringing about any change on the ground, I would suggest them to be more patient as the issue is too complicated in scope and depth to be solved by some individuals or organizations. It requires collective effort from the individual level to the community level to the national level and to the international level with the interest solely for the benefit of the humanity. His Holiness has been doing his part as an individual to affect some change in this direction using his influence as a globally recognized leader.

To counter the analysts who have pointed that His Holiness is not a pluralist in the real sense of the word,I would say that he has never claimed to be so as he is a Buddhist to the core. He is a realist in his approach to resolve religious conflicts which is to emphasize on the similarities rather than differences. The philosophical or doctrinal questions of ultimate truth, after life, previous life, genesis of life, origin of life and the like have different answers in the scriptures of different religions. Focusing on them will only divert our attention from what matters to us to live in happiness, i.e. love, compassion, forgiveness and tolerance. It is said that many a time, even the Buddha ignored these questions posed by his disciples and drew their attention of to the path of love and compassion. The pluralist approach to religious harmony ignores the simple fact that the religious leaders of the major religious traditions like Christianity, Hinduism, Islam, Buddhism and Judaism are deeply devoted to their respective philosophies and doctrines embedded in their age-old scriptures which some believe are revealed by the God. Nothing can even this out. Nobody can uniform them. Communists tried to do it with own 'religion' but failed. I believe that His Holiness is in the right position to rally the religious leaders of the world to be united to spread the universal message of love and compassion while respecting the philosophical differences of their respective religions which are the result of differences in dispositions and conditions.

For quite a long time since I first came across the three commitments of H.H.The Dalai Lama, I had a confused skepticism over the other two commitments preceding the last one which is to find a resolution of Tibetan cause. I have often asked myself with an omnipresent guilt as to why his commitment to our struggle for freedom comes last. But I have realized that only a selfish nationalist ignorant person like me can have such doubts because he is not just the spiritual and temporal leader of six million Tibetan people but is the Buddha of Compassion for not just 7,800,000,000 human beings but innumerable sentient beings.

A lay man of a great political stature cannot bring the leaders of these great religions together to lead them. A lay man of a great military power can crush these pillars of great religions but cannot destroy their foundations. Only a religious icon like His Holiness the XIVth Dalai lama is the beacon of hope.

CHAPTER FIFTEEN

What Do Animals Talk About?

Cast of Characters:

1. Hen
2. Cow
3. Pig
4. Street Dog
5. Sloth
6. Domestic Dog

Scene: In a dense forest

Hen: (*huffing...*) Where am I? Where should I go? Will they catch me? (Hears rustle.) Who is there? Who is there? (*The cow appears through the trees.*)

Cow: (calmly) It is me. Don't be scared. (*The hen is petrified)* Calm down.

(*In the meantime, the pig appears sniffing around oblivious to the surrounding. Both of them are scared.*)

Pig: (*bumps into the cow..and snorts*) Who are you two?

Hen and Cow: We are we. And who are you?

Pig: I am me.

Street Dog: (*hidden in the bush..*) Don't you know your names? What do you mean: I am me, We are we? (*The dog clears through the bush..*) Do you even know what a name means?

Sloth: What is there in name? Names are for name's sake.

Street Dog: (*feeling offended..*) Who are you? You are stinking.

Sloth: I am the stinking sleeping sage, the sloth. My mind is single pointedly concentrated on sleeping.

Street Dog: Where are you?

Sloth: I am invisible to your eyes. I have become the tree on which I meditate.

Street Dog: What do you mean?

Cow: Strange fellow...

Sloth: I can hear you. I am not strange. I am just telling you the truth. Reality is the product of perception. I am invisible to you because you can't perceive me as through life long meditation on sleep sticking to the tree my outer appearance has metamorphosed into the tree.

Hen: Where are we?

Sloth: You are home.

Pig: What? We ran away from home. This does not look like the place where we lived.

Cow: Yeah..

Sloth: This is your home. This is where you belong. This is where your kith and kins are. This is the home of your ancestors.

Cow: What is the place I lived in?

Sloth: It is the place where humans grow you to eat you.

Pig: No....They are very good to us. They feed us. They take care of us. They even clean our shits.

Cow: I have never seen them eating us.

Hen: Yes, they are very kind to us. There are thousands of us in our place. Sometimes I wonder how they can manage us all.

Street Dog: They steal your eggs. They steal your milk. They are fond of your juicy fat.

Cow: You are talking non sense. Actually when they milk me, I feel relieved. The bulging udder is a burden for me. I don't need them.

Sloth: It is meant for your calves, but they don't let you raise them. They deny you of your motherhood. And they have even deprived you of your male partners.

Cow: Male partners? What are they?

Street Dog: The ox. They were used to till their land for agriculture when they were not depended on machines. You needed your male partners to make babies. Now humans do it for you.

Pig: I have never met mine too.

Hen: Me too.

Sloth: Yes, because they don't want to waste their resources to rear your male partners just to make babies with.

Hen: But how do we make babies with our male partners?

Sloth: Forget about it. I can't show it to you. You have to see it. If you live in the jungle, you will experience it. It is beyond your comprehension as you don't know even how your male partners look like.

Street Dog: I have seen your male partners chewing plastic bags in the middle of the streets in the city, where I am from.

Cow: How do they look like?

Pig: How do they do it for us?

Street Dog: You stupid pig, they do it for them with their machine. They called it artificial insemination.

Sloth: They have used us. Now they are using machines. They are not going to stop until they destroy themselves with their machines.

Pig: I don't mind what they do to me as long as they feed me and clean my shits.

Street Dog: Didn't you escape from the farm?

Pig: No, they were taking us in the back of a moving thing. Out of curiosity I jumped out of it and fell on the street and bruised myself. See this.

Street Dog: Good. You are lucky. You literally jumped out of hell. They were taking you to the slaughter house, where you would be killed to be turned into ham, curries, meatballs etc. So, the bleeding bruise you have got is just a scratch compared to what could have happened to you if you had not escaped from the small truck, the moving thing.

Sloth: Your kinds are also placed on their plates to satisfy their appetites. Some of them don't eat us.

Cow: Why?

Sloth: Some don't eat you because some of their gods ride on you. Some don't eat you because you are considered filthy.

Hen: What about me?

Street Dog: You are eaten by everyone who eats meat. None of their religion restricts eating you.

Hen: What? This is not fair. Isn't my life as valuable as her(cow)? Doesn't any of their gods use me for their transportation?

Street Dog: No, but your dead body is more expensive than theirs. A kilogram of your carcass costs more than theirs.

Pig: How is it so? It does not make sense to me.

Sloth: You thick skinned. Simple economics: higher the demand, higher the price. There is a direct relationship between the two. Actually we, wild animals, are more civilized than the civilized humans. You know why? Long time ago, humans used to hunt for food. They took what they needed from nature. Now, greed governs them. They domesticate you in a large number confining you in their prison. You are killed in a large number and store your carcass in their cold storage for tomorrow. They have complicated philosophies, but they don't follow even simple ones. They know they are doing wrong, but they just tinker around it. They can see the danger. They can analyze it. They can eliminate it, but they don't. They evade it and put it off for posterity with philosophical resignation.

Street Dog: We wild animals fight for food and survival. Humans kill one another not only for food and survival, but also to keep their belief alive. For example, they have put a ban on killing, selling and eating of your species (cow). You (hen) are most preferred. They don't have any guilt eating you, but they don't like to see you butchered in the filthy corner of their shop. I have never seen you (pig) alive in their shop. I have only seen your chunks of mutilated body on display.

(*something ruffles in the bush*)

Hen: (*anxious*) What is it? Something is in the bush?

Street Dog: Who is there? Come out.

(*a domesticated dog appears*)

Who are you?

Domestic Dog: My name is Pink Pampered.

Pig: He looks like you, but you are shabby.

Street Dog: He is a slave to his master. I have freedom.

Domestic Dog: My master does not treat me like a slave. He loves me. He feeds me, cleans me and walks me.

Cow: You are not as skinny and dirty as he. I think your owner treats you well.

Domestic Dog: He is not my owner. He treats me like a friend.

Sloth: Humans can be no one's friend. Believing that they can be our friends is wishful thinking. The basis of their relationship is need or greed. Earlier they kept dogs to guard their house and to herd their cattle. Now- a- days they keep you to comfort them, to fill the hollowness inside them, to satisfy their need for companionship. They are so lonely in their crowded cities. Their modern technology has replaced their ancient need for you. They don't need you to guard their house and herd their cattle. You are just your owner's lap dog and their status symbol.

Domestic Dog: We are friends. He doesn't own me.

Street Dog: What is on your neck?

Domestic Dog: Band.

Street Dog: What is it for?

Domestic Dog: To fasten my leash. Don't you know that, you loafer, vagabond, wanderer....

Street Dog: I am not tied to a leash like you, but to liberation.

Domestic Dog: Freedom means nothing when you have to constantly worry about food and shelter. My friend provides both to me. That is freedom to me. I am free from fighting for food, females and family. I am protected.

Street Dog: You are so pathetic, but you can't do what you want to and when you want to. You have to dance to his whims and fancies. Fighting for food, females, family and frontier is the way of life of real dogs. You are just like one of their toys to play with.

Sloth: Enough...Nobody is free.

Cow: Even humans?

Sloth: No, they are worse than us. They are entangled in their own mind whereas we live by instinct which is in tune with nature. Yes, we fight for food and family. Our future is uncertain. So is theirs. We are better off than them because we don't have what they call monkey mind. Our life is simple.

Hen: But I wish I were humans.

Sloth: So that you could eat chicken?

Pig: or Pork?

Cow: or me?

Street Dog: Humans are strange. They even fight over whether they can eat one of us or not.

Hen: Except me?

All: Ha..Ha....

(*They hear gunshot....*)

Cow: What was that?

CHAPTER SIXTEEN

Hitler And Bose

Cast of Characters:

1. Adolf Hitler
2. Subash Chadra Bose
3. Hitler's Secretary
4. Hitler's General
5. Bose's Secretary

Scene 1:

Hitler's office is well furnished with a broad table behind which his armchair stands. There are chairs in front of the table. The Swastica sign hangs on the wall on top of which is his portrait with the Nazi salute.

(Secretary is flipping through some files. Hitler enters.)

Hitler's Secretary: (*with the Nazi salute*) Hail Hitler!

Hitler: (*returning the salute*) What business do I have today?

Hitler's Secretary: a couple of appointments, Fuhrer.

Hitler: Who am I meeting first today?

Hitler's Secretary: The General to discuss about your meeting with Subash Chandra Bose.

(There is a knock on the door. The General enters with the Nazi Salute.)

The General: Hail Hitler! (*takes his sit*)

Hitler's Secretary: (addressing the *General*): Fuhrer would like to hear about your views regarding the meeting with Subash Chandra Bose.

The General: Of course. What I want to discuss with you is in exchange of freeing India from our enemy British, the independent India should help us invade Tibet.

Hitler: Why invading Tibet is important?

The General: To stop Russian influence in the area. We need to step in first. India can be our military base to expand our empire in Asia.

Hitler: With our ally, Japan, we can conquer the whole world.

Scene 2:

(There is knock on the door. Bose enters with his secretary.)

Bose: (*greets Hitler with namaste and handshake*) It is my pleasure to meet you finally.

Hitler: I have been looking forward to meeting with you.

(Bose greets the general and takes his seat)

Hitler: Are you fine? You look very frail.

Bose: I am fine, but it has been a very long and arduous journey to meet you. I have been under the British surveillance for a long time. They have been tracking my every movement. I have become the master of masquerading to escape them. They have got an inkling of my meeting with you. So, it is impossible to take the sea route to Europe. I had to travel through Afghanistan and Greece to Europe in disguise. It took me three months.

Hitler: That's an amazing feat. It shows your grit and determination. You can definitely free your country from the imperialist British.

Bose: That's my aim, but it is possible only with your military help.

Hitler: Of course, we are ready to help you fight our arch enemy. We are friends. Tell me about your plan.

Bose: I have formed Indian National Army. We have been recruiting men and women to mobilize our force to oust the Britishers. We have around 100000 men and women ready to sacrifice their life. But we need modern arms and ammunitions. We can't fight them with just bows, arrows and crude weapons. We need air force too. We plan to form our base in the Nort East Frontier of India which shares border with Myanmar. Your ally Japan has control over it.

The General: If I may interrupt Fuhrer. Fuhrer is ready to help you, but we have a pre-condition.

Bose: We are prepared to negotiate.

The General: In exchange for our help to free your country from British, you have to help us to invade Tibet. We have been trying to establish contact with them. But they have not shown any interest. Russians are doing the same. Britishers already have their trade posts in Tibet after invading it in 1904.

Hitler: Apart from the geo-political advantage of making Tibet as our ally, my interest lies in its spiritual and esoteric power. Our scientists have the capability to harness the energy of an atom to build the most powerful bomb the mankind has ever known, but I want more than that. I want to be immortal. I want to get access to Shangrila where the beings live blissfully eternally. My aim is to weaponize the esoteric power of Tibet to free the world from the evil axis of allied force.

Bose: (suppressing his chuckle) I don't have any intention of being immortal. I want to die for my country.

Our ancient scriptures also mention the use of weapons as powerful as the sun in the battles of Mahabharata, but I seek your immediate military help to fight the Britishers who have ruled us for 200 years. It is urgent that we fight them with might.

Hitler: But what about Mr.Gandhi. Does he approve of your tactic?

Bose: no, he does not nor his Congress Party. Therefore, I have resigned from the party. They believe that Britishers will leave India in peace. But there is a large section of people who believe that in addition to nonviolent movement, our country needs to confront the British with military force. I respect Mr. Gandhi for his dedication and commitment to his principles and his nonviolent actions. Afterall both of us want to free India. And I can assure you that if India is freed, we can be your ally to free the world from the British and French colonialism. Asia and Africa need to be freed from them.

The General: Yes, you are right. And we can establish the reign of Aryans in the whole world. Hail Hitler!!! Hail the third reign!

Bose: I hope you are not talking about world domination or a new empire.

Hitler: No, definitely not. We only wish to establish a new world order instead of the present one.

Bose: I agree with you. We need a new world where I vision India playing a crucial role. I vision India not only to have the cultural strength, but also the economic and military power so that she will never be under the subjugation of another country.

The General: We have missed an important issue here, Fuhrer.

Hitler: What is it?

The General: What about the invasion of Tibet?

Boss: But Tibet is already free. It has not colonized any other country. It is nation of peaceful people. Does it need to be freed?

CHAPTER SEVENTEEN

I Am Ozymandias, The King Of Kings

Cast of Characters:

1. Ozymandias, the great pharaoh of Egypt
2. Zubane, the guide, female, an Egyptian
3. Mark, the tourist, Egyptologist.
4. Sam, the tourist, gay, an American

Scene: *A vast stretch of desolate desert with a lonely weathered statue of Ozymandias, Ramses II, the pharaoh of Egypt. The guide and the tourist are on a camel ride in the desert.*

Zubane: We are half way through the journey to the mysterious lake.

Mark: Does it even exist?

Zubane: Yes, it does. I was lucky to come across it when I was travelling with my father on this way. He had a caravan of goods to barter in the city. So, whether the lake exists or not depends upon your luck. (*With a sarcastic tone and wry smile*) The sand hides many secrets.

Sam: How old were you then?

Zubane: 15.

Sam: (*with disbelief*) That is reassuring! So, we are guided by a guide who is guided by the map-less luck. (*suddenly a cloud of dust appears*) (*with fear*) What is that?

Zubane: (*with anxiety*) Oh! The dust storm. Can't you see? How come we did not notice it? We need to get down the camels and hide behind them.

(*They are caught in the whirlpool of the wailing storm.)(When the storm settles......*)

Mark: Sam, where are you?

Sam:(*in muffled voice*) I am under the sand behind the butt of my camel.

Mark: (*looks for Sam*) Where are you?

Sam: Here...

Mark: Are you o.k.?

Sam: I am fine except the smell of the camel I am wearing. (They hear Zubane)

Zubane: Are you two fine?

Mark and Sam: (*together*) Where are you?

Zubane: I am here. (*They extract him buried under the sand.*) (*After some time...*) I can't believe what has just happened. The storm just came out of the blue without any warning. It could suggest that something bad is going to happen.

Mark: Don't be superstitious. It is just a natural phenomenon for which we don't have a scientific explanation.

Sam: (*with awe...*) Look! What is there in the back? A statue!

Mark: What statue is that, Zubane?

Zubane: I don't know. I have never heard of it. (They observe the statue with admiration.)

Sam: Wow, it is so huge. Whose statue is it?

Zubane: Never heard of it. It is a bad omen.

Mark: Don't be silly, Zubane. Look, something is inscribed on the pedestal.

Sam: What does it say?

Mark: It is written in ancient Egyptian language.

Zubane: Can't you read it? You are the only Egyptologist among us.

Mark: I know this ancient language. It is written in hieroglyphs. It says, "My name is Ozymandias, king of kings: Look upon my works, ye Mighty, and despair!"

Sam: I don't know anything about him, but it seems that he was conceited and arrogant. Well, let us take a picture with the king of kings.

(*Takes the picture. With flash, the statue comes alive.*)

Ozymandias:(*with suspicion*) Who are you all?

(*All of them are speechless and awestruck.*)

Mark: I am Mark. He is Zubane and he is Sam.

Ozymandias: Where am I? What am I doing in the middle of the desert?

Zubane: You came alive when we took the picture of you.

Ozymandias: (*with contempt*) You don't take picture of someone. You draw their picture. So, where is my portrait?

Sam: Here, in the camera. (showing him the camera.)

Ozymadias: (*with contempt and disbelief*) Are you trying to fool me? Where is the canvas?

Sam: Look at yourself in the monitor. (*shows him*)

Ozymandias: That is a statue of me. Not me.

Mark: You were a statue before we drew the picture of you with this thing.

Ozymandias: I can't believe such a thing exists. Who are you? (*pointing at Zubane.)*

Zubane: I am a fellow Egyptian. My name is Zubane. I brought them here. I am a tourist guide.

Ozymandias: What is a tourist guide?

Zubane: They are here to take a tour of our country. And I am paid to guide them. They are from a foreign country.

Ozymandias: What do you do? (*pointing at Sam.*)

Sam: I am photographer. I draw pictures without brush and colour.

Ozymandias: No, you are not a pho..to...grapher. You are a magician. Anyhow why are you wondering around in underwear? You are shameless. This is sacrilege. In my palace, for many generations, the job of people like you is to entertain our wives.

Mark: Where are you? Don't you know you are in future? The world has changed a lot.

Ozymandias: Time changes, not the custom.

Zubane: Yes, things have changed a lot. You are no more a king.

Ozymandias: What do you mean? I am the king of kings, not just a king. I am the great Ramses II. I have expanded my empire and built temples, cities and palaces. Don't you know that?

Mark: Yes, we know. Your greatness is buried in history. You are nothing now. Just a while ago, you were just a neglected forgotten broken statue.

Ozymandias: Don't try to fool me. You strange people. I don't know where you are from and I don't know how I got here in the middle of the desert.

Mark: This is where your great empire was. Now what you see is just the great expanse of desert. So, you are nothing. Time has defeated you. Nature has destroyed you. Whoever sculpted you was not fond of you. He has mocked your arrogance and conceit in the face of your statue. See it is imbedded in you. You still carry those expressions of on your face. You are remembered today for your cruelty.

Ozymandias: I couldn't have expanded and secured my great empire without cruelty. Every great king has been cruel and violent. Otherwise, we would still be living in tribes and clans. There would not be countries and empires and civilizations. Cruelty is a necessary evil.

Zubane: But, we Egyptians in our history referred to you as Userma'atre'setepenre, which means Keeper of Harmony and Balance, Strong in Right. You are our Great Ancestor. However, it is sad to say that our region which had a glorious past is in unending crisis. Syria, against which you lead three military campaigns and failed to defeat your enemy, Hittites, but had to sign the first ever recorded peace treaty in the history between two nations, is embroiled in internal conflict. It is under the siege of a rebel group called ISIS. Innocent people are suffering as they did during your time. Foreign powers are pulling the string for their vested interest. And our country Egypt is in debt. People are unemployed. We are in economic crisis. The situation is similar to the great plague which struck Egypt. In fact, the cruel reality is that the glory of Egypt is gone.

Ozymandias: I can't believe what you all are saying. All of you are trying to fool me. All of you are making up this story. But you might be true about my death. I remember dying. I died of old age. I lived for 90 years and ruled for 67 years.

Sam: And this magical box brought you alive. I brought you alive, but you insult me. Even though you are alive, you are just an ancient artifact. If you want to live in the 21st century, you need to change your attitude towards women and transgender like me.

Ozymandias: (*dismissing*) Anyways, can you sell the magic box to me? So that I would never die though we believe that death is a gateway to immortality, but I don't remember anything after my death.

Sam: But you have nothing except the cloths on your body. You are as poor as a pauper.

Ozymandias: Ha..ha...don't you know our custom? Mark, you are an expert on our civilization. My wealth is safe in my tomb in the pyramid where I was mummified for next life. You can imagine how rich I am. I can not only buy this magic box, but also you as my slave to entertain me.

Mark: But, the pyramids have been looted by treasure hunters and excavated by archeologists. Most of the remains of your ancestors are in museums for display. Your mummified remain is in Cairo Museum. It has been thousands of years since the civilization your dynasty had created has gone into dust.

Ozymandias: It is unbelievable...Oh...no...What should I do now? Where should I go now?

Zubane: I can help you. But you have to earn your livelihood. Do you have any skill?

Ozymandias: No, except martial skill. I can fight war.

Zubane: But you are too old to join the army. Moreover, these days they don't use swords and spears and chariots in war. They use guns, bombs, drones and other weapons of mass destruction which is beyond the range of your imagination.

Ozymandias: I don't understand half of what you are saying. So, what can I do? What if I told them I am the great pharaoh?

Sam: Children will laugh and make fun of you. Ordinary people will think you have gone crazy. Psychologists will presume that you are delusional suffering from some mental disorder.

Ozymandias: So, what can I do for living?

Sam: Nothing..You are good for nothing. You should have learned something other than fighting. The great Ramsis II is unemployed! But there is a job for you.

Ozymandias: What is it?

Sam: Your condition is very suitable for this. Can you beg because you are poorer than a pauper? Even a beggar is richer than you.

Ozymandias: What? I would rather be a broken colossal statue than an disgraceful beggar. Can you please turn me into the broken statue with your magic box?

Sam: This is not a magic box. It is a camera. Let me see if it works. Let us take a selfie with the flash on. (Takes the selfie.)

Ozymandias: Have I turned into the statue?

Sam: Touch yourself. Have you? What do you think? You can stand here thinking that you are a statue. You know the power of imagination.

Ozymandias: oh..what should I do now?

Zubane: Don't worry. I will guide you to be a guide like me. But, you have to be my assistant. You have to choose a career to live your life.

Ozymandias: O.K..but how can I ? You are a woman. How can I work under you?

Zubane: Since you can't be changed into the statue, you have to change your ancient attitude. Your are not alone, there are still men with the mummified mentality like you in our country.

CHAPTER EIGHTEEN

We Are Not Broken

Adapted from the story 'Two Gentlemen of Verona' by A.J.Cronin

Cast of Characters:

1. Nicola, the elder brother, who is 13 years old
2. Jacobo, the younger brother, who is 12 years old
3. Cronin, the narrator
4. Jane, the Nurse
5. Waiter, works at the café

Scene: *The scene is near a café with a table and four chairs around it.*

Nicola and Jocobo: (*In hurry*) thank you for the drive, Mr.Cronon. Wait for us at the café. We will be back in an hour.

Cronin: Boys...where are you hurrying to?

(*Cronin gets in the café, takes a chair and checks the menu*)

Cronin: Excuse me....excuse me. (*Calling out to the waiter*)

Waiter: Good afternoon, sir. What can I get for you?

Cronin: I would like to have a cup of black coffee.

Waiter: (*Notes down*) anything else?

Cronin: What can I get which goes well with the coffee?

Waiter: Well, I recommend you the specialty of our town. It is special cheese cookies baked in our traditional oven. You will not find such cookies anywhere except at this café.

Cronin: I would like to try some, but if I don't like them...I am not going to pay for them. Ha..ha..ha..

Waiter: Ha..ha..ha...No.... You will love them so much that you will ask for more and end up paying more! O.k. I will get your order soon. But it will take some time to bake the special cookies. We serve them fresh right out of the oven. So, here is the today's news paper to give you company.

(Cronin goes through the newspaper. After some time, the waiter returns to the table with the order.)

Waiter: (*cheerfully*) here you are, sir!

Cronin: Hmmm....the cookies smell great! Thank you very much.

(After a while...)

Cronin: Excuse me...excuse me...

Waiter: (*keenly, running towards him*) Yes sir...

Cronin: Can I have another cup of coffee? And....(*with a mischievous smile)* the cookies were great.

Waiter: I told you so. You will love them. So, are you going to have some more?

Cronin: No, absolutely not. I don't want to pay more! Ha..ha..ha...just kidding, my friend. Yeah, I would love to have some more.

Waiter: I will be right back....of course..... after some time.

Cronin: Wait...by the way......is there any good place to hang around? I have another half an hour to wait for those kids.

Waiter: Well...there is nothing much to see here except the debris of the buildings destroyed in the war by the enemy. Just around here, there was a 5th century catholic church, which was a big tourist attraction. Now, you will find its glory buried under its rubbles. Anyway, we have beautiful mountains which adorn our desolated town....but half an hour is not long enough to get there!

Cronin: Well.. What is that villa?

Waiter: Oh..that is....(*Meanwhile, Jane enters cutting in the conversation between them)*

Jane: Excuse me. Can I join you?

Cronin: (*surprised*) Oh! Sure....you are welcome. (*With an awkward smile, offers her the chair.)*

Jane: Thank you. (*She takes the chair*). Sorry to disturb you like this, but I saw you with the two boys through the window (*points at the villa*). How do you know them?

Cronin: Well....by the way I am Cronin.

Jane: (*in embarrassment*) Oh...excuse me...I forgot to introduce myself. I am Jane. I work there. So, are you their relative?

Cronin: No, I am not. I came here to drop them. I am a tourist from America.

Jane: I see. Then, how do you know them?

Cronin: I met them in Verona, where I have been staying for the last few months. Next Monday I am going back to my country.

Jane: Well...What do the boys do there in Verona? I have always wondered. But I have never asked them. I believe that they must be doing well.

Cronin: They do different kinds of work there.

Jane: Aren't they doing anything wrong? I believe they don't.

Cronin: No, in fact I am very impressed by them. I admire them for what they do.

Jane: What do they do?

Cronin: Hmmm...They do many things. They hawk fruits, shine shoes and show visitors around the places of interest and run errands They proved extremely useful to us. We totally depended on them in getting a pack of American cigarettes, reserving seats for the opera or recommending the name of a good restaurant. We could rely upon them for anything we wanted. They work very hard day in and day out in the hot sun and the cold night.

Jane: I can't believe it. They are so young.

Cronin: Yeah, but they have matured beyond their age. What strikes me most is their willingness to work.

Jane: How did you meet them?

Cronin: When I first met them, we were driving through the foothills of the Alps on the outskirts of Verona. They stopped us to sell wild straw berries. Though my driver told us that we would get fresher straw berries in the city, my companion and I bought the biggest basket. There was something about them which attracted us to them.

Jane: Where do they live in the city? Do they have any apartment?

Cronin: I don't know. One night, we came upon them in the windy and deserted square, resting on the stone pavement beneath the lights. It was midnight and they looked tired. A bundle of news paper lay at Nicola's feet. They were waiting for the last bus from Pauda to sell their remaining papers. So, it seems that they don't have any shelter except the public square to spend their night. But, I am not sure, as I have not asked them, because I did not want to offend their self esteem. They seem to be very proud of themselves especially Nicola. When Jacobo asked me a favor to drive them here, Nicola was hesitant to accept my help. I felt that he did not like the idea.

Jane: Poor boys... How cruel fate is! At least, they have their family legacy of pride with them.

Cronin: Has something horrible struck them? They must be wounded deeply. Because even though we have become friends, they haven't told me about their family. When I asked them what they did with the money they were earning from their hard work. They just told me that they had some plans.

So, I wonder what they do with the money they earn there. It seems to me that unlike other street children who work with them, Nicola and Jacobo don't spend any money on themselves, as they just wear tattered clothes and eat black bread and figs only. What has happened to them?

Jane: Poor boys... They are the victims of the horror of the war. The plans they are working so hard for is to pay the bills for the treatment of their sister.

Cronin: (*surprised*) Sister? They did not tell me about her. They just said that they live here and visit their family every month. Do they live here?(*Pointing at the villa.*) When we arrived here in my car, they jumped out of the car, and told me to wait here and disappeared beyond the corner of the wall of that villa. The villa is magnificent. I am surprised because I did not expect that they live here.

Jane: (*amused*) No...no.... they don't live here. It was donated by a wealthy family to the Red Cross to use it as a hospital after the war. This place was badly bombed by the enemy. The government hospital was overcrowded with the people injured in the war. Their sister is also admitted here.

Cronin: (*surprised*) what for?

Jane: She has been suffering from spinal tuberculoses.

Cronin: How did that happen?

Jane: Her spine was badly injured. She did not get the treatment on time as the government hospital was overcrowded. Moreover, when she was brought here, she was malnourished.

Cronin: Who brought her here?

Jane: Her brothers.

Cronin: What do their parents do?

Jane: Poor kids...They are orphans. Their mother died when they were born. Their father who was a popular musician raised them all by himself. He was training his daughter to be a great singer. They were the envy of the whole town as they were well off and cultured. But the war destroyed their life as that of many of us. He died in the rubble of their house bombed by the enemy. So, they had no shelter and food for months. They lived in a ramshackle hut made out of the rubbles of their bungalow. They survived on roots and wild fruits. And their sister was left without treatment.

Cronin: On our way here in the car, when Nicola was putting out his shirt, I saw a deep scar on his right shoulder. It looked like a bullet mark.

Jane: Oh...that must be a bullet mark. During the three years of the enemy occupation, their hatred for the enemy grew. So, they, as many young boys like him, joined the resistance movement to fight them. In fact they were the first to join the resistance movement. So, Nicola and Jacobo were underground when they were supposed to be at school. They had guns and grenades in their tender hands instead of pens and pencils. Now, their hands are busy doing odd jobs in the city. They are deeply wounded by the war but you can't see them. You can only sense them in their eyes. You too must have. The war has carved a path of hardship for them.

Cronin: And when did they bring their sister to the hospital?

Jane: When the enemy left, they came back for their sister, who was afflicted with the T.B of spine by then. They brought her here. It has been 12 months since then. By god's grace, she is getting well. Every month they pay their bill and visit her. Poor boys.... they are all by themselves. There is no one to help them. But they seem to be doing well compared to hundreds of homeless young men and women, who have lost their ways. Since our economy is also in shambles, everything is scare: jobs, food, water; electricity...The war has deprived us of even our basic necessities of life. So, these young men have taken to crimes and the young women to prostitution. There is degradation all around. There is no money to educate them. War is a curse to humanity.

Cronin: You are right. But, isn't the government doing anything?

Jane: No, we have a government for namesake. As soon as the enemy left, our country was engulfed in civil war. The very resistance groups which fought together against the enemy fought against one another! The enemy could destroy everything except our spirit. But, the civil war has destroyed our spirit as well.

Cronin: So, who run the government?

Jane: A bunch of criminals, I would say. Corruption has seeped into every fabric of our society. Hopelessness reins us. Desperation commands us. Bleakness leads us.

Cronin: Can I help in any ways? (*with an ironical smile*) I am in a better position because our government made lots of money out of the misery of the people. During the war, our military industry boomed while millions of homes in other countries were bombed and doomed. Our government sold killing machines to the murders of humanity. I am really ashamed of my own country.

Jane: Sir, don't blame yourself for what your government has done. You are as innocent as we are. We don't have anything to do with any war. We are victims of our own people and our enemy. However, people like you restore our faith in human goodness. It is very kind of you to offer us help. If you like to, you can help us to provide free medical treatment to those who can't afford. There are many families, whose family members are critically injured and it is extremely hard for them to pay the bill. As you know we had to charge those young boys also. We are desperately in need of financial aid. But, we can't rely on the corrupt government.

Cronin: I promise when I get back, I will raise fund for the hospital. And personally I would like to pay for the treatment of Nicola and Jacobo's sister.

Jane: That is so kind of you. It will ease the burden off their young shoulders.

Cronin: But I have a condition....

Jane: Please tell me. What is it?

Cronin: Please don't tell them about it. I respect their self dignity.

Jane: O.K....I can understand.

Cronin: Oh...Sorry...I forgot to order for you. What would you like to have?

Jane: Just a milk coffee.

Cronin: Excuse me....

Waiter: What can I get for you, sir?

Cronin: A milk coffee for madam.

Waiter: O.K...(*Runs back to the kitchen*)

Cronin: By the way, how old are they?

Jane: Nicola is elder. He is 13. Jacobo is a year younger. Why don't you meet their sister? Don't you?

Cronin: I would like to, but I don't want to intrude into their privacy. 'They prefer to feel that they have kept their secret. Yet their devotion has touched me deeply. War has not broken their spirit. Their selfless action has brought a new nobility to human life, has given promise of a greater hope for human society.'

(After a while, the two boys come to the café. From the outside, Nicola calls the nurse with hesitation.)

Nicola: Mrs. Jane...Please, come here. (*She comes out.*)

Jane: What's the matter?

Nicola: Have you told him about us?

Jane: No...I have just come here. Do you know him?

Jacobo: Yeah...He is a tourist from America. He brought us here in his car. He stays in the hotel where we work.

Jane: (tauntingly) Oh...you work in a hotel. You never told me.

Nicola: (playfully) You never asked us. So, why should we?

Cronin: Hey boys!!! What are you doing there? Get in.

Jocobo: O.K, sir, we are coming.

(*They get in the café.)*

Nicola: Sir, sorry for keeping you long.

Cronin: It's O.K. No problem. I had a great time here.

Nicola: Sir, this is Mrs. Jane. You must have introduced one another.

Cronin: Yeah...We have just met.

Jacobo: She looks after my ailing mother at home. (*Jane throws a surprised look at him*)

Cronin: Where do you live? You two just disappeared beyond that wall.

Nicola: Oh...we have a big bungalow behind the wall.

Waiter: Madam...here is your coffee.

Cronin: Hey boys...would you like to have something before we go back to the city? It will get dark on the way.

Nicola: No, thank you very much sir, we have had a sumptuous meal cooked by our sister. She is a fine cook. Since our mother got sick, she has been taking care of our home.

Cronin: (*jokingly*) You did not tell me that you have a sister.

Nicola: (*jokingly)* You did not ask us, did you?

Cronin:*(with love*) Your father must be proud of you boys.

Jacobo: (*with a sigh, scratching his head*) Yes, he is.

CHAPTER NINETEEN

'Soepa'

Scene:*In mosquito netted double bed. Two windows in the front and left of the bed, a table fan fixed on the wall in the background, a messy coffee table on the right and a small table in the corner between the bed and the wall in the front. On the right are metal almirahs against the wall.*

Cast of Characters:

1. Soepa, husband
2. Ngawang, wife
3. Tsewa, their daughter

Soepa: (*slapping her mouth)* shut up! Shut up! Shut up!

Wife: (*sobs, resists*) don't do this in front of her (Tsewa)

Soepa: (*slaps her harder restraining her hands with his left hand*) shut up your fucking mouth..shut up.

(*She sobs. Tsewa cries. He gets out of the bed and sits in the chair.*)

Soepa: (*soliloquy*) Bitch, she deserves it. She needs to be taught a lesson. She needs to know who the man is. It is me, not her. She can't dominate me. She can't boss around. She needs to know I am the man. What does she think of me? (*He keeps quite and reflects.*) Oh, shit! What did I do? I hit her. What went wrong with me? It was not me. What has happened to me? I feel so bad. (*He goes to the bed. She was still sobbing. He holds her from behind and kisses her neck and asks her forgiveness.*)

Ngawang: Leave me alone.

Soepa: Please, forgive me. I am sorry.

Ngawang: (*pushes him*) Leave me alone.

Soepa: Sorry. I mean it.

Ngawang: Your sorry is meaningless.

Soepa: Don't say that. When I am violent, I don't mean to harm you. But I really mean it when I ask for your forgiveness. I really feel very bad.

Ngawang: Do you think I can't hit you back? If you think so, you are wrong. I can, but did not because I don't want to do it in front of our daughter. You have become shameless. You have changed.

Soepa: Yes, I feel ashamed of myself for my behavior lately.

Ngawang: Don't think that I am scared of you.

Soepa: Why would you say that? Why don't you ask me what the matter is? (Tears well up his eyes. He feels a lump in his throat.) You know I love you, but I am acting insane. (Ngawang keeps silence.) You never talk to me about what is going on with me. When I am messed up, you just remark that I have changed.

Ngawang: Yes, you have. You don't care about me anymore. You have got what you want.

Soepa: You always say that. But you know I did not insist on it. I did not want it.

Ngawang: Even if you didn't want it, you have got it.

Soepa: You know why I got so pissed off. Before we came here, I told you not to create any drama. When you came out of the Bata shop and complained I looked very tense and no smile on my face, I got really angry and scolded you, because just earlier our baby ran through a narrow gap between auto rickshawas to the crowded traffic. I ran towards him but my backpack got stuck. That's why I was tense. Moreover, you had to walk so long in the heat. You are not supposed to do that in your condition. At the mall, when you said you wanted to have some snacks, nobody listened to you, not even your mother. It was understandable that your brother did not understand, but your mother is supposed to know. I felt everybody was there for their own sake. I wanted to say something, but I did not.

Ngawang: Why didn't you? You should have.

Soepa: I could have, but I thought I should not because the atmosphere was already tense because while looking for the optician shop where your uncle got his glasses made, your brother was very bitter at your uncle. He was shouting at him.

Nagwang: It is not a big deal.

Soepa: But I am not used to it. It is not normal to me. And you also yelled at your uncle when he wanted to go his way. Why do you all treat him like that? There is double standard in the way you tre at him and other uncles. Why is it so?

Ngawang: I don't know what you are talking about.

Soepa: Don't pretend. You know exactly what I mean. Is it because he is dependent on you? Is it because he has no children and no money?

Ngawang: Don't talk none sense.

Soepa: See. You don't talk. You don't express. You just vent out.

Ngawang: Now, you have started again to scold me. You never talk to me nicely.

Soepa: Judge me by my action. You like being sugar coated.

Ngawang: Yes, I do. I need somebody who can understand me.

Soepa: So you think I don't understand you.

Ngawang: Yes you don't.

Soepa: You are true I don't understand you. You accuse me of being changed, but actually you are. Since the birth of our children, you seem to have changed. The way you behave with me is different from earlier. You have started treating me like a punching bag as you do with your mother. I don't know why you are acting like that.

Ngawang: I don't know what you are talking about. I have not changed at all.

Soepa: Yes you are. You seem to be irritated all the time. You are moody.

CHAPTER TWENTY

Philanthrophy

Cast of characters:

1. Samphel, husband
2. Wangmo, wife
3. Dhondup, Samphel's friend

Scene:*a bed against the wall in the center; a tv set on the left and a coffee table in the front of the bed. A wall clock and an alter.*

When the curtain opens, the phone rings. Samphel is lying on the bed reading a book.

Samphel: (*picks up the phone and talks to himself*) Whose call is it? Looks like an international call. (*He receives the call.*) Hello, who is it?

Dhondup: Tashi delek, it is Gyaltsen. (*the voice was crackling*)

Samphel: Oh! Tashi Delek. How are you? What's up?

Dhondup: Tashi Delek. I am fine. So, how is everything?

Samphel: Everything is fine here.

Dhondup: It has been a long time since I called you last time.

Samphel: Yeah, but it is ok. These days, you get to know how your friends are doing on Facebook. Ngawang Tashi used to call me and a couple of times he asked me if I had Facebook account. It was 4 years ago when I did not have the account. I check your Facebook timeline, but yours is mainly political.

Dhondup: Yeah, you know I am into photography. Whenever, H.H. arrives here I am the official photographer. I am planning to put up an exhibition of the photographs I have taken.

Samphel: That's great. Put some on Facebook too so that we can also appreciate your art.

Dhondup: That should not be any problem. I will send you an invitation to visit Austria. It is a beautiful country. You should visit it. If you pay for travelling, we can arrange the rest while you stay here.

Samphel: It sounds good. Thanks. But, we can't afford the flight. You know we are government servants and ours is a refugee school. We earn enough for a decent life, but we can't expect foreign tour, a car or a house of our own. And we have to save for our children's higher education. (*Wangmo comes and gestures to know who I was talking to. I cover the phone and whisper to her, 'Dhondup.' She contorts her face and leaves.)* You know up to class XII, we don't need to worry about our children's education, as it is free of cost, but college education is very expensive. Even though the government provides scholarship, it is not enough. If your child wants to pursue some professional degree, the fees are very high. Recently I came across an article in a magazine which says that the cost of higher education will be higher. After a decade, taking into account the rate of inflation, the professional courses like engineering, doctor, MBA, etc. will require at least Rs. 40 lakhs.

Dhondup: Sometimes, I feel I shouldn't have disrobed. I should have stayed in the monastery. Life is o complicated now. When I was in monastery, it is not that I was free from worry, but considering how things are now, life was very simple. But you know I guess this is what they mean when they say that grass is always greener on the other side. Anyways, you know if you come here, you don't need to worry about your stay and tour in our city. By the way, how is Lhakpa?

Samphel: He is fine.

Dhondup: How is his son? I have not called him for ages, nor has he.

Samphel: His son is fine. He has started to go to nursery.

Dhondup: (*In a teasing voice*) when are you going to be father before you start planning for your children's education?

Samphel: I am planning, but I am not sure. I will be father sooner or later. There is no hurry. Once you have a child, your life changes. They become the number one priority of your life. Isn't it? You have the experience!

Dhondup: Yeah, you are right. But, don't be late! I guess you are waiting for the right person.

Samphel: Not exactly. I am too lazy even to wait in this matter. I believe I will come across who I find interesting. So far I am not interested in those who are interested in me. However, I haven't taken the vow of celibacy like you did.

Dhondup: Don't pull my leg!

Samphel: On Facebook, I saw your photographs taken in Tibet. The scenery was breathtaking.

Dhondup: That was my hometown.

Samphel: Finally, you got the visa.

Dhondup: Yes, but the official at the Chinese embassy made a lot of fuss about my visa application. You know I have been quiet active politically here. My photos of 10th March commemoration march have been in Austria's popular news paper. Moreover, they have checked my background in India. They knew that I was a former monk in the monastery, which has been the most politically active monastery in Tibet. Many self immolators are from our monastery.

Samphel: May be finally they are satisfied that you are not potentially as harmful as they thought. We are not free in a free country. You are bonded to your wife, chained to your children and enslaved to free market forces. So, did you all visit Tibet?

Dhondup: Yes, we did. Actually, we planned to have our friends with us. But it did not work out.

Samphel: How were your parents?

Dhondup: They were fine.

Samphel: You met them after many years. It must have been a great experience.

Dhondup: Yeah, they were very happy to see me, but I was saddened to see the kids wasting their life. There isn't any school in the area. They expected me to help them financially. So, these days, after work, at weekends and festivals, I sell momos to collect fund. I have been very busy.

Samphel: That's great, but why don't you form a trust and seek the help of others too from your hometown?

Dhondup: It is not difficult to form a trust and get it registered, but it is very complicated.

Samphel: So, you want to do it on your own without any external pressure. There are many NGOs with noble goals in Dharamsala, but it seems that they formed them for self-employment. They entitle themselves with fancy posts and perks doing nothing much.

Dhondup: Yes, you are right. We, Tibetans, are fond of forming self-serving groups. I think we haven't got rid of tribal instinct.

Samphel: So, what are you collecting the money for?

Dhondup: For school building in my area.

Samphel: But, aren't they nomads? They keep on moving. I think it is better to help them financially to buy books and to pay the teacher who can move with them. A mobile school! It is easy to build a concrete structure. However, to keep it running, you need dedicated staff and good curriculum.

Dhondup: Yes, they are nomads, but not their children. They stay with their grandparents at their permanent homes. So, I have seen them loitering around wasting their time.

Samphel: Aren't there any school nearby? In India, at a certain distance in every village there is a school.

Dhondup: Yes, there is one set up by the Chinese government, but it is quiet far away and parents don't prefer to send them there. Only grandparents stay at home. They can't manage.

Samphel: Why don't you finance building a hostel for them near the school and the cost of running it?

Dhondup: No, I am thinking of a day school for them with the community so that they can be with their grandparents.

Samphel: It is a great idea. You need to be very determined and dedicated. I wish you all the best. Actually it is a very difficult task. It is not just financing. There are lots of other things.

Dhondup: Yeah, I know. By the way, when are you going to be a father?

Samphel: I told you I am not in hurry. You know life changes once you have a baby. Your child becomes the center of your life.

Dhondup: Yeah, making a baby is not as difficult as raising them. But, you are lagging behind.

Samphel: Yeah, but I am not in race. It will happen sooner or later. Do you remember you used to ask me when I was going to get married? I gave you the same answer. It will happen when the time comes. (Dolma comes and raises her eyes and gestures to express her surprise.)

Dhondup: (laughs) But it is time now, my friend. Do you remember the volunteer lady teacher? She was asking me about you. She wants to get married with a Tibetan guy.

Samphel: Yeah, I remember.

Dhondup: She said she was there actually to find a suitable husband.

Samphel: What? I can't believe it.

Dhondup: Many of them visit Dharamsala looking for peace and a peaceful Tibetan husband.

Samphel: ha..ha.. Are you a peaceful Tibetan husband to your wife?

Dhondup: What do you mean?

Samphel: Just kidding, bro! How is your wife and children?

Dhondup: They are fine. Actually, I wanted to ask you if my children can get admission to TCV School.

Samphel: Why? Are you migrating back to India?

Dhondup: Hey, stop pulling my leg. Actually my wife wants to study Buddhism at the Library and Tibetan Work Archive. She wants to be a translator here at the monastery. At present she is doing odd jobs.

Samphel: So, I guess you all are going to stay here for long.

Dhondup: Yes, we are.

Samphel: How long?

Dhondup: At least two years.

Samphel: Great, regarding the admission, you won't face any problem. You have to pay fees even though your children are from a father, who was a nomad when he was in Tibet and in exile a monk. But now you are from a developed world.

Dhondup: Ha...Ha...You enjoy teasing me. So, what is the procedure? Can you do it for me?

Samphel: Bro, I wish I could. But I am not in Dharamsala. I am in Dekyiling. But, the procedure is not complicated. Go to the head office in upper TCV. The concerned authority will help you.

Dhondup: Where should he get the admission?

Samphel: It depends upon where you stay. If you stay in Mcleod Gunj, there is TCV day school. If in lower Dharamsala, there is Lower TCV and Peton Lobdha.

Dhondup: What is Peton Lobdha?

Samphel: It is run by Sambhota School Administration under Department of Education. It is an experimental school where the medium of instruction is Tibetan unlike English in other Tibetan Schools. It is said that students from this school are better in English than those from English medium Tibetan schools.

Dhondup: How is it so? It doesn't make sense to me?

Samphel: It is said that if a student has a good command over their mother tongue, it is easier to be proficient in a second language. Moreover, I guess teachers, especially English language teachers, are well trained. And the class is also small and manageable.

(Wangmo points at the wall clock with an irritating look.)

Samphel: Anyways, what are you doing these days?

Dhondup: Nothing, just babysitting. They are on vacation. My wife is at work. It is better to stay at home and baby sit than hire a baby sitter to go to work. Baby sitting is expensive. What about you? Are you writing anything?

Samphel: No, I am just reading a lot. I am not ready for it.

Dhondup: You should as I always tell you. I will be more than willing to finance the publishing of your book.

Samphel: Thanks, I will definitely, but not now. Well...I have to hang up now.

Dhondup: O.k

Samphel: Let me know if I can be of any help to you.

Dhondup: O.K. Bye.

Samphel: Bye.

(After some time, Wangmo comes.)

Wangmo: Who was that?

Samphel: Gyaltsen.

Wangmo: Oh, you guys talk so long like lovers.

Samphel: Ha..Ha...

Wangmo: How is he doing?

Samphel: He is doing well. You know finally he was able to visit his parents in Tibet after more than 20 years.

Wangmo: 20 years! I can't believe.

Samphel: There are many from Tibet who are separated from their parents. He is the fortunate one. Those who are refugees in India can never see their hometown in Tibet.

Wangmo: Why so?

Samphel: Unless they cross the border illegally because they don't get visa from the Chinese embassy as we have chosen to be registered foreigners in India unlike Tibetans in the west where they acquire the citizenship of the host country.

Wangmo: This is not fair. Why can't we be Indian citizens?

Samphel: We can, but we will lose the privilege of free education for our children, free settlement to live in, and freedom to choose our representative in the parliament in exile and so on.

Wangmo: But Tibetans in the west apply for citizenship of the country they have immigrated to. Do they lose their privileges as we do?

Samphel: No, except that they have to pay fees if they want their children to study in a Tibetan school in India.

Wangmo: That doesn't make sense. Why would they send their children to India to study when students here compete to study abroad?

Samphel: Yes, you are right. Some of them send their children for summer camp to learn Tibetan language and culture. If they want to visit Tibet they can as they can apply for visa because they have pass ports, but we in India can't. I have been reading a book called A Home in Tibet by Tsering Wangmo Dhompa, who lives in Sanfransisco. The book tells you about her people and her father's birth place. It is beautifully written. I felt like visiting Tibet like her, but I can't.

Wangmo: (She sighs.) By the way why did your lover call you? He must have some favor to ask you.

Samphel: Yeah...That's how it is. All relationships are need based.

Dolma: What? I don't need you.

CHAPTER TWENTY-ONE

Butter Lamp

Cast of Characters

1. Choebul, a monk who has self-immolated
2. Pamo, Choebul's mother
3. Phuksam, Choebul's father
4. Samten, a close friend of Choebul

Scene1

In Choebul's room. Bed at the back in center. A table in the right corner. On the wall the portrait of H.H.The Dalai Lama hangs. He is in bed attended by his mother.

Choebul: (*confused and in pain*) Where am I?

Pamo: At home. Thank god....you are conscious now.

Choebul: Am I not dead?

Pamo: No..my son.....you were in comma in hospital for a week. The police let us take you home because the doctor told them that you won't make it. You are badly burned.

Choebul: (*with difficulty in breathing*) What happened to Lhaksam? Is he dead?

Pamo: Yes he died on the spot.(*sobs*)

Choebul: (*with a sigh*) He achieved his goal. I should have been dead. I don't want to live under such a repression.

Pamo: Son, please don't say so. We are glad that you are alive. (*knock on the door*) It must be pala. (opens the door) Pala, our son is out of comma!

Phuksam: Really, thank god. (*rushes into the room where his is. Sobs..*) Son, how do you feel? Thank god. You are back.

Choebul: I am fine, pala. But I should have been dead. Better to be martyr than be oppressed by the moron.

Phunksam: No, son. You can serve our cause better by being alive than dead. It is fortunate that you did not succumb to the burn.

Choebul: Have not they bothered you?

Phuksam: the police.

Pamo: yeah, they want you under their custody. They are charged with colliding with the dalai clique. Your pala has been interrogated many times. They want to know your accomplices.

Phuksam: yeah, they were very rude. And I have been suspended from my job indefinitely. I don't know what they want to know.

Choebul: Pala, I am really sorry for causing you this trouble.

Phuksam: don't worry. Actually I admire you now. In the beginning I was angry and shocked at what you did.

Choebul: Why haven't they taken me?

Phuksam: I bribed the chief officer, who I am acquainted with.

Pamo: greedy dog. It cost us almost all our fortune. (knock on the door) Who could it be? I will get it. (*She exits.)*

Phuksam: I am glad that you are out of comma by god's grace. You should take some rest.

Choebul: Ok, pala.

(*Pamo enters with Samten, a friend of Choebul. He greets Phuksam.*)

Phuksam: you two catch up with one another. I will go to the market for shopping. We will celebrate tonight. Samten la stay for dinner. Amala, get some tea for them.

Samten: But pala, it is better if people don't know the present condition of Choebul.

Phuksam: Yes, you are right, but they come here every day to check his condition.

(*After they leave, Choebul and Samten are alone.*)

Samten: Choebul, how are you?

Choebul: (*with a tone of regret*) I am alive. What happened to you? Why have you disrobed? (*with surprise*)

Samten: I left the monastery recently. Since you self immolated, our monastery has been under police surveillance for 24 hours. I could cope up with the restrictions, but could not bear their demand to vilify H.H.the Dalai Lama. They gave us a choice either to disrobe or vilify our tsawey lama.

Choebul: I am sorry to hear that. My sacrifice has been good for nothing except to cause trouble to our monastery. I prefer death than to be alive in their prison.

Samten: Your sacrifice has not been in vain, but you should not stay here. You should flee to India to let the world know what is going on here. People say that it is useless to lose your precious life for our cause because nobody cares. The international media has been dump. They say they are not allowed to enter Tibet, but that is just an excuse. They can if they want to. However, you can make a big difference to the movement if you get out of here.

Choebul: Is it possible?

Samten: I can arrange for you. I know a person who can help. He helped me to return from India.

Choebul: You never told me about that before.

Samten: I have kept the secret to hide my identity.

Choebul: Who are you?

Samten: I had been in India for twenty years. I studied Buddhist Philosophy at Drepung University in India. I have received Geyshey Lhamrampa. My birthplace is Taktser in Amdo.

Choebul: I can't believe it. You have been at our monastery for two years. What are you doing here?

Samten: I could not go back to my home. I have been away for more than twenty years. They will suspect me for a spy of Tibetan Government in exile. One of my friends in India who came back to his home was arrested and has disappeared. His family believed that he has been tortured to death.

Choebul: But why have you returned after such a long period of time? You should have stayed there.

Samten: (*with hesitation*) Mmm.........I missed home. Moreover, most people pay lip service to our cause. They are lost in the humdrum of their life. What occupies their mind most of the time is how to get to America or Europe. People don't feel that they are refugees because they don't face the hardships that other refugees have to bear. (with a sigh) Anyways, you should flee to India. If they get to know that you are out of comma, they will arrest you. They will ask you who prompted you to put yourself on fire. Well....have you been encouraged to take that step?

Choebul: No, I acted on my own. It is because of their mental atrocities committed against us. I have not colluded with anyone. (with sarcasm) How can we? We don't have that freedom. Who do they think I have connection with?

Tibetan Government in exile or Tibetan Youth Congress?

Samten: It is an embarrassment for the Chinese government. They can't believe that these are individual acts of defiance against the repressive policy of the Chinese government.

Choebul: How are political prisoners treated in India?

Samten: The government treats them well. In general, people respect them, but many are cynical of political prisoners. It is said that there have been cases where some people from Tibet who claim to be political prisoners were actually imprisoned for penal crimes. They lie so that they can avail the opportunity to settle abroad. You know political prisoners are given political asylum in Australia and Europe.

Choebul: Then would they believe that I immolated myself?

Samten: You and other martyrs are looked upon in India. You all are the true heroes after Pawo Thupten Ngodup. They have been demanding the Chinese government to send you to the U.S for medical treatment. They are inspired by the sacrifices self immolators like you have made for Tibetan freedom.

Pamo: (with tea) Samten la, have some tea. (*She sits beside her son.*)

Samten: Thank you, ama la.

Choebul: Amala, is not Pala back?

Pamo: No, he is not. He will be back soon. What is the matter?

Choebul: Amala, Samten says I should escape to India. I can be safe there.

Pamo: You should. We don't know what is going to happen to you once they know that you are out of comma.

Choebul: Do you think pala will let me? You know he did not let me go to India for education when I was younger when our uncle advised him to do so.

Samten: But, now he would. Your life is in danger. You can't stay here. You will be either life imprisoned or executed without any trial.

Pamo: Yes, Samten la is right.

Choebul: But, I don't want to and pala will also not like the idea.

Pamo: Why? What can you do being here except being imprisoned?

Choebul: Those who escape to India can do nothing much. They have the freedom to shout slogans, but nothing else. What can they do abroad except creating awareness and raising slogans? Many doubt their intentions also.

Samten: So, what is your point? What can you do here?

Choebul: I can be their inspiration. Being executed or behind the bars for life is better than being chained to the hum drum of life.

Samten: Yes, our struggle desperately needs ordinary people leading the path to freedom. We need ordinary heroes.

(*Banging on the door....*)

Pamo: Who is it? It is not Pala. Let me check. It must be Chinese Police. Keep quiet. Choebul, pretend that you are still in coma. (Amala leaves to open the door.)

Chinese Police Officer: Why did it take you so long to open the door?

Pamo: Sorry...I did not hear.

Chinese Police Officer: How is the charred dog doing?

Pamo: He is still in coma.

(*The officer enters Choebul's room. Palmo goes to the kitchen.*)

Chinese Police Officer: (suspiciously) Who are you?

Samten: I am Samten. I am his friend.

The Chinese Police Officer: Where are you from?

Samten: Amdo.

The Chinese Police Officer: What are you doing in Lhasa?

Samten: I am at my Uncle's. I was a monk in Drepung monastery.

The Chinese Police Officer: Why have you disrobed?

Samten: It is better to be a layman.

The Chinese Police Officer: What do you mean by that?

Samten: There is more freedom. I am not restricted by my vows.

The Chinese Police Officer: That's true. How can you live your life in that prison? Show me your ID. You said you are from Amdo.

Samten: Yes, here it is.

The Chinese Police Officer: O.K....how well do you know him? Did he ever tell you about the self-immolation?

Samten: No, he did not. I was shocked to hear the news. Since I left the monastery, we have not been in touch with each other.

The Chinese Police Officer: You are lying.

Samten: No, I am not. You know I am an ex-monk.

The Chinese Police Officer: ha...ha....are you trying to pull my leg?

Samten: No..no....sir.

(*In the meantime, Phugsam finds the door ajar, enters calling out his son with excitement.*)

Phugsam: Choebul, my son. Amala, we are going to celebrate tonight.

(*While saying so, he enters the room. There was dead silence.*)

The Chinese Police Officer: (*suspicious*) What are going to celebrate for? You called out the name of Choebul. Is he out of coma? (*looking at Pamo*)

Pamo: No, he is not.

Phugsam: No, he is not. I did not call out his name. How can I? He has been lying in the bed like a dead body. We are going to celebrate because Samten la, who is a friend of my son, has visited us. He too is like our son.

The Chinese Police Officer: Are you trying to fool me? (*stands up.*) Guards, hold up. (*He holds his neck.*) Do you think I am a fool? Tell me the truth. (*pushes him on the ground and turns towards amala and slaps her.*) You, rotten liar, tell me the truth.

Choebul: (*removing the medical support system*) I will tell you the truth. Being in political comma is worse than being in medical comma. Your government has been trying to put us in comma for the last 60 years. We want to show you the pain inside us by burning ourselves up. But you can't see. You rob us in clear daylight and claim to end the darkness of our history.

The Chinese Police Officer: You shut up, charred dog! Guards take him.

Phugsam: Please, sir. Pardon him. Can I talk to you aside?

The Chinese Police Officer: There is nothing to talk about? All of you are traitors.

Phugsam: I beg you. Just for a minute. (*Takes him to the other room.)*

Pamo: Spare us, please.

The Chinese Police Officer: What is it? Hurry up.

Phuksam: Please don't arrest him. Nobody knows except us that he is out of comma. So, can you please not inform about this to your higher authority?

The Chinese Police Officer: I can't do that unless your offer is irresistible. You know I am a greedy communist. I have already done you the favor of not taking him under our custody. More than half of what you gave me went to the higher authority.

Phuksam: How much do you want?

The Chinese Police Officer: Depends upon how much you value your son's freedom.

Phuksam: (*aside to audience)* I wish we could buy the freedom of our country from the Chinese leaders, but Xi Jing Ping would not allow, as he is hard against corruption. What can I offer him? (*To the Officer*) Sir, wait a minute here. I need to talk to my wife.

The Chinese Police Officer: Make it hurry. By the way, I am coming back after sometime. I have to raid a house. He is suspected of ties with the Dalai clique.

Scene 2

(Pamo enters Choebul's room.)

Pamo: What happened?

Phuksam: He agreed to keep it from the higher authority if we grease his palm.

Pamo: How much? How can we? We have already paid lots of money to him to let Chebul's stay with us.

Phuksam: I have no idea what to do.

Samten: Can I be of any help?

Pamo: Really????

Samten: Yes, I can.

Phuksam: How will you do that?

Samten: I can't tell you that. I have my sources.

Choebul: My friend, don't bother yourself. If they find out you will be in trouble.

Samten: They won't.

Choebul: Actually I don't want to hide here or flee to India. I have not committed any crime. It is my country. They should hide from us or flee to China.

Samten: You should escape to India. I have some contacts. If you are alive and free, you can do a lot for our cause.

Choebul: Yes, I want to, but in Tibet. You told me that political prisoners can't do much abroad. What can they do with the freedom they have? What freedom? Free to raise slogans: Tibet belongs to Tibetans, Go back China....But now, to appease the Chinese government, protestors are instructed to restrain themselves from raising such slogans. I know only two slogans: 'Free Tibet' and 'Invite H.H.The Dalai Lama Back to Tibet.'

Pamo: Son, we beg you to escape to India. They will execute you.

Phugsam: In the past, I did not send you there with your uncle, but this time you should, it is a matter of your life.

Choebul: I will never.

(There is knock on the door)

Pamo: Who is it?

Phugsam: It must be the Police Officer and his men.

Other Titles By The Author

Moments: Love Loss and Longing, his debut book which is a collection of poems, won International Excellence Award in 2023.

www.ingramcontent.com/pod-product-compliance
Lightning Source LLC
Chambersburg PA
CBHW031735150726
47989CB00006B/2463
* 9 7 9 8 8 9 5 8 8 0 6 4 7 *